W9-BIN-675

What people have said about Steve Clapp and Fred Bernhard's *Widening the Welcome of Your Church*

"This book revolutionized the way we relate to visitors and is fueling a new wave of growth in our congregation. This is the most practical book I've read on making the church into the kind of community that embraces new people."

United Methodist Minister

"Thanks for this wonderful book. Our adult and youth Sunday school classes all studied it, and it's transforming our church."

Church of the Brethren Minister

"Bernhard and Clapp provide practical ideas that can increase the quality of hospitality. . . . This book has great value for pastors and the entire church."

Herb Miller in *Net Results*

"Christian Community provides a wealth of resources that should be made available to local churches. This book is current, to the point, and easy to read."

Ivan George, American Baptist Churches

"This is a very practical book that will help local churches who are serious about their caring and about their outreach."

Loren Mead, Founder of The Alban Institute

"Our church has never been comfortable talking about evangelism, but the hospitality approach fits us very well. Studying this book has helped us learn how to do outreach in a way that fits our congregational culture."

United Church of Christ Minister

About Fred and Steve's book
Hospitality: Life in a Time of Fear

"The best benefit from studying this book has been the difference made in the personal lives of study participants. This book teaches you how to look at the world through the eyes of Christ."

Lutheran Minister

"This book gave a new perspective to me and to many in our church. Hospitality can transform how you drive, how you relate to clerks in stores, how you live with your family . . . "

Episcopal Church Minister

"This valuable new release deals directly with the tough questions raised by the tragic events of September 11, 2001. . . . recognizing the presence of Christ in others can have a liberating impact on all we do." *Church Educator*

"The book can be used by pastors who must deal with the undercurrent of fear in our society. . . . and church leaders who simply want to make their church more hospitable to strangers." *Net Results*

"This book will help you find meaning and purpose in a fearful world and equip people to extend healing and hope to others living in fear."

Sheila Hoover in *Leadership Development*

"How can the church function in an environment of fragmentation, violence, and fear? This book takes a practical approach, offering many excellent suggestions to congregations grappling to show hospitality in our complex time."

Mennonite Weekly

Deep and Wide:

Hospitality and the Faithful Church

Steve Clapp, Fred Bernhard, & Ed Bontrager

A LifeQuest Publication

Deep and Wide: Hospitality and the Faithful Church

Steve Clapp, Fred Bernhard, & Ed Bontrager

Copyright © 2008 by LifeQuest.

All rights reserved. No portion of this book may be reproduced in any form or by any process or technique without the written consent of the publisher, except for brief quotations embodied in critical articles or reviews.

For further information, contact: LifeQuest, 6404 S. Calhoun Street, Fort Wayne, Indiana 46807; DadofTia@aol.com; (260) 744–5010.

Biblical quotations are from the New Revised Standard Version of the Bible, copyrighted 1989 by the Division of Christian Education, National Council of Churches and are used by permission.

ISBN-10: 1–893270–43–2
ISBN-13: 978–1–893270–43–5

Library of Congress Control Number 2007933511

Manufactured in the United States of America

Contents

Chapter Six
Children, Youth, and Young Adults

Concept: Virtually all churches talk about the importance of having children, youth, and young adults involved; but we need to become more intentional about truly assimilating people of these ages into congregational life.

Chapter Seven
Entry Points and Deeper Relationships

Concept: There are many different entry points into the life of a congregation, and all of them are important. Regardless of the initial point of entry and the initial experiences in the church, people will only continue to come if they have been helped to develop and maintain deeper relationships with God and with one another. Even long-time members can have experiences that alienate them from the congregation.

Chapter Eight
Creating Healthy Churches

Concept: There are no canned programs or quick fixes that will create the climate of hospitality in your church that will result in members who readily reach out to the unchurched and who can effectively assimilate new people into congregational life. Hospitality must run through the whole fabric of the congregation rather than simply being a welcoming "program," and the making of disciples must be a top priority for the church.

This book is dedicated to:

- All those persons whose love and caring have helped assimilate new people into the body of Christ.

- Paul Mundey and our other colleagues in New Life Ministries who confirmed the need for this book.

- The staff of Christian Community who made the book a reality.

- Lyle Schaller, who wrote the best book ever on assimilation (and on several other topics as well).

Our special thanks to Kristen Leverton Helbert, Stacey Sellers, and Holly Sprunger for their help with this book and to all the clergy and congregations who have cooperated with Christian Community on research and pilot projects. We are thankful for the work of our friends at Evangel Press and for their high standards in book production.

For just as the body is one and has many members, and all the members of the body, though many, are one body, so it is with Christ. For in the one Spirit we were all baptized into one body—Jews or Greeks, slaves or free—and we were all made to drink of one Spirit. Indeed, the body does not consist of one member but of many.

1 Corinthians 12:12–14

Chapter One
Sylvester, Handshakes,
and Expanding the Community

1 Corinthians 12:12–31

Concept: Hospitality when people start attending is very important, but deeper hospitality must happen for people to truly become part of the community of faith.

Steve and his wife Sara have had either two or three pets for most of the time they've been married; but following the death of their beloved dog Jolie, they were down to a single cat, three-year-old Grace. At first they thought they would stay with just one pet for a couple of years. Then they noticed that Grace increasingly seemed bothered, indeed downright depressed, when they had been gone even for a few hours; and she was almost in mourning by the time they returned from a vacation. Both of them work, and Steve's work involves considerable travel. They started talking about the possibility that they should get another cat to be a companion for Gracie.

About a month later, they discovered a black-and-white cat spending a lot of time hiding under the hosta plants in their yard. The hostas were conveniently located by their bird feeder; and they assumed that their visitor was an indoor-outdoor cat who lived in the neighborhood and who was interested in eating their birds. Grace is strictly an indoor cat, posing no danger to any outdoor creatures and not in danger herself from cars or other animals. Since their purpose in feeding the birds was not that of providing meals for cats, they started chasing the visiting cat away when they saw him.

Then one afternoon Sara, who tends to be more observant than Steve about these things, pointed out that this cat was very thin and had a matted coat. "I don't think he belongs to anyone," she said. "He's hunting birds because he's hungry." And there was no evidence that he had ever successfully caught a bird, so he was probably exceedingly hungry. Sara decided to start calling the cat Sylvester, after the cartoon cat, because of his black-and-white coloring and because he tried, apparently unsuccessfully, to catch birds.

So they decided that putting out food for the cat would be a way to keep him from hunting birds. He ate the food they put out, but he remained very skittish and ran off whenever they got at all close to him. Early one morning, however, he seemed to reach the conclusion, as several people have, that Sara was a nicer and safer person than Steve; and he actually let her pet him. He became increasingly friendly and in time let Steve pet him as well.

They started asking themselves if Sylvester was somehow a sign from God. Had God sent this cat to them precisely at the time they were starting to wonder if they wanted another pet? Or had God implanted the idea of a second cat in their minds at the time this one was ready to wander into their lives? Or were they making up a theological justification simply because they were starting to get attached to this cat?

Obviously there are continuing signs of God's presence in the world around us. The whole created world and all the living things that are part of that world are signs of God's creative activity. The prologue to the Gospel of John reminds us of the reality that the creative power of God, called there the Word of God, became flesh in the person of Jesus Christ. Jesus Christ stands as the foremost sign of God's presence in the lives of past, present, and future generations.

And the Word became flesh and lived among us,
and we have seen his glory, the glory as of
a father's only son, full of grace and truth.
John 1:1–14 [NRSV]

Then Paul's letters in the New Testament present the concept that in the church, you and I become part of the body of Christ. Christ is the head of the church, but we become part of Christ's body when we join the Christian community. As a result, there is a very real sense in which you and I are signs to one another of the presence of God in our midst.

Deep and Wide Hospitality

The sharing of the good news of Jesus Christ and the expansion of the community of the church should be central to our lives as Christians. Yet there are still significant numbers of people in North America who are not part of the life of any congregation, even though large numbers of them in fact believe in God. Some of those persons have belonged to a congregation in the past but have no desire to be part of one now.

Finding accurate statistics on this is difficult; but the best estimate from research by Christian Community, the organization for which Fred Bernhard and Steve Clapp work, is that at least half of those who are not affiliated with any church or other faith-based institution at the present time have been a member or an active constituent of a church at some time in the past. They have *chosen* not to continue that involvement.

Within a year of officially joining a congregation, 62% of those members are *less active* in the church than at the time they joined. Twenty-five percent simply stop coming within

the first year of official membership. Those figures come from current Christian Community research and hold true across denominational lines. The consequences of this add up year after year. Some become reactivated, but others remain uninvolved or leave the church by their own choice. Some inactive members are eventually removed from the membership rolls when churches are seeking to clean up their records. There are some churches in which more than half the congregation is essentially inactive except for an occasional appearance at Easter and Christmas.

As people of faith, many of us are concerned about bringing more people into the life of our congregations and about sharing what our faith in Jesus Christ means to us. But we have not done a particularly good job of fully integrating large numbers of people into the life of our congregations.

All three of the authors of this book have written extensively about the topic of hospitality, but **we have increasingly been feeling that the level of hospitality in our congregations just doesn't go deeply enough to connect with people at a level that will keep them coming and isn't wide enough to help newer members really feel that they are as much a part of the community of faith as longer-term members**. We also have the problem of negative experiences happening to people once they have become part of the life of the church, and those experiences can drive them away for years.

Let's go back to the story of Sylvester. Did God send that cat to the Clapps' yard precisely at the time that they were thinking about the possibility of getting another cat? Or did God plant in their minds the idea of getting another cat in anticipation of Sylvester appearing in their yard. Or does God really get into that much micro-management? Perhaps the truth is that God didn't directly engineer what happened but that they had the obligation, as with other matters in life, to determine what should be done.

As you probably suspect, Sylvester worked his way from the hosta plants to meals on the back porch into the living room. The progression in his status, however, wasn't without problems. They had a large veterinary bill to get his shots, to get rid of his fleas, and to take care of neutering. The initial flea treatment was less than 100% successful, resulting in continued treatments of both Grace and Sylvester and the spraying of the entire house.

Steve and Sara may have thought they were taking Sylvester into the home as a favor to their cat Grace, but Grace spent months in less-than-full agreement with that decision. Sylvester learned to be aggressive to protect himself as a homeless cat, and he proved a bully with Grace, especially where food was concerned. There was also competition for affection between the pets. Grace developed a preference for Steve, and Sylvester developed a preference for Sara.

Over a period of time, with a lot of work and a lot of patience from Steve and Sara, things began to improve. Sylvester developed greater security that there would always be food in his bowl and stopped being so aggressive. Grace seemed to go through a program of assertiveness training and started lightly whacking Sylvester on the head when he did something that annoyed her! And when both cats decided that there really was enough affection to go around, they started interacting more positively with each other. Now they play together and frequently sleep close to each other. Grace no longer acts depressed when Steve and Sara are gone, which was one of their original hopes.

Sylvester is successfully integrated into the Clapp household and has certainly proven himself a blessing from God to Steve,

Sara, and Grace. But maintaining positive family dynamics, even in a house with only two humans and two cats, is not always an easy process.

And maintaining a high quality of congregational life in which everyone feels affirmed and valued is also not always an easy process. It can feel to clergy and to church leadership like a congregation with 300 active members has 300 different opinions on some topics! People who feel affirmed and excited when they join the congregation may over a period of time start to feel that they don't really belong. Many factors can cause that including these:

- **They may start to feel that their opinions are not as valued as those of some others in the church.** Devin was an enthusiastic new member of a church and had strong ideas about how the property of the church should be managed. He was appointed to the board of trustees, who were responsible for the church property, and quickly learned that others had their own ideas. He wanted a plain, subtle pattern for the new carpet in the sanctuary, but others on the board decided to go with the bold, more striking pattern that an interior designer recommended. He felt that a particular company would do the best job replacing the church's aging boiler, but the rest of the trustees decided to go with a company that had a lower bid. Devin began to feel that his opinions just did not carry as much weight as those of some others.

- **They may not have enough significant interpersonal connections with others.** The lunch invitations that they received as potential members don't keep coming, and they suddenly realize that they do not have the close friends they thought they did. Andy and Beth joined the church in large part because they felt such a close connection with the pastor and his wife. They went out to dinner as guests of the pastor and his wife once, treated the pastor and his wife themselves, and then were guests again in the pastor's home. But after they had joined the church, they began to realize that the pastor and his wife were extraordinarily busy and did not have time for frequent social engagements with Andy and Beth. Building relationships with other couples in the church seemed to go slowly, and they finally stopped coming. If meaningful relationships had been formed with more people than the pastor and his wife, they would no doubt have felt differently.

- **They may have had unrealistic expectations about what it would mean to be part of a congregation.** They may not adequately understand that it is impossible for a large number of people to all have their own way on many church decisions. That was part of Devin's problem. And it was also part of the problem for Andy and Beth, who thought they had a level of friendship with the pastor that would continue. The pastor in fact continued to feel very good about Andy and Beth, but the evenings he and his wife reserved to be with other couples were used primarily to reach new people for the church. Devin needed help understanding how decisions had to be made in a large congregation, and Andy and Beth needed stronger connections with other people in the church—not just the pastor and his wife.

- **They may find that their personal faith and beliefs differ more from those of others in the congregation than they had realized.** Sometimes

15

when the hospitality of a congregation is exceptionally high, people may overlook or not notice differences in beliefs that later become important. Courtney and Blake were delighted by the high level of warmth at St. Matthew's, and they found the minister to be a very dynamic speaker. The music was great, and they felt strong connections with people in their Sunday school class. After they had been members for about a year, however, they began to notice that the pastor and people in the Sunday school class were strongly opposed to the war in Iraq. Courtney came from a military family and had grown up in a church that always backed the country in any conflict. The church began to feel unpatriotic to her, and she realized that the peace emphasis was a major part of the theology of the denomination to which she now belonged.

- **There can also be times when someone in the church does or says something that is directly hurtful.** Nate and Bethany were happy in the life of their new church home and were especially happy that their son, who had a learning disability, seemed to be fitting in. Then a frustrated Christian education teacher spoke sharply to Bethany, saying, "Your son behaved badly again. He talks out of turn, and he isn't cooperative. And he's also one of those who runs down the aisle at worship for the children's story instead of walking like he's supposed to. I think you need to exert some firm discipline with him and straighten him out." The teacher who spoke those harsh words had been through a bad week herself and thought she should apologize the next week. But there was no next week, because Nate, Bethany, and their son did not return. Obviously discipline issues can be a problem that must be addressed in church, as in other settings, but the approach used makes a tremendous difference.

Not as Friendly as We Think

Christian Community has carried out membership surveys on over 1,600 congregations around North America. In that process, they've learned some interesting things about the way we actually practice (and fail to practice) hospitality in our churches. The following chart contrasts responses between the national average and the average in congregations that are growing for three important survey items.

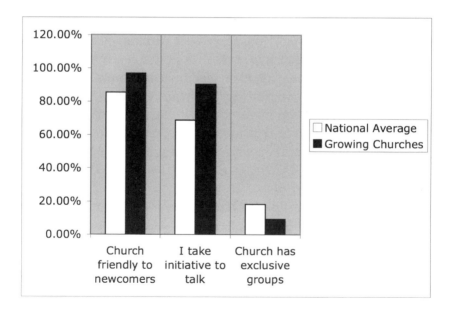

The first pair of bars contrasts responses to this statement: "In our congregation, people go out of their way to be friendly to strangers and newcomers." Most people in most churches think that the congregation is friendly. The national average of persons agreeing or strongly agreeing on this item is 85.4%, but the average in growing congregations is higher at 96.9%.

A more significant change begins to show in responses to a more personal item: "At church, I take the initiative to talk with those I do not know well." The national average of persons agreeing or strongly agreeing on this item is 68.7%, quite a bit lower than the percentage feeling that the church is friendly to newcomers. In growing congregations, however, 90.4% of those responding agree or strongly agree with this item. People in growing congregations are considerably more likely to take the initiative on reaching out not only to newcomers but also to anyone in the church they do not know well. This makes a tremendous difference in the atmosphere of the congregation.

Far too many congregations have defined hospitality in a way that equates it to smiles and handshakes for visitors. Certainly smiles and handshakes are nice, but that doesn't go nearly far enough. Fred Bernhard had a conversation with a person who described his congregation as very hospitable. Fred asked how that hospitality was demonstrated. The person responded, "If a visitor shows up and we get to them, we'll invite them to our home for a meal." Fred asked, "What do you mean, 'Get to them'?" The response was, "If they are still around after we've visited with everyone else." That, of course, is not real hospitality. Real hospitality takes far more initiative and seeks to treat guests with preference.

But what happens when people are no longer guests but are part of the community of faith? How accepted do they feel then? The third comparison in the chart concerns whether or not people feel excluded: "In our congregation, there are cliques or exclusive groups which can make one feel unwelcome." The national average of agreement with this item is 18.3% with the much lower percentage of 9.3% in growing congregations agreeing with the item. There are some very troubled congregations in which the percentage agreeing with that item climbs to as high as 68%.

And how compassionate do people perceive the life of the congregation to be? The survey includes an item related to that: "In our congregation, people care for one another in a way that is more compassionate than what I have experienced in other groups." The national average of persons in congregations agreeing or strongly agreeing with that statement is 75.9%. That seems fairly high, but remember that it means almost a fourth of those responding do *not* feel that care in the congregation is more compassionate than they have experienced elsewhere. And if care within the Christian community isn't perceived as more compassionate than elsewhere, what is wrong?

The percentage agreeing or strongly agreeing with the statement about compassionate care in growing congregations is 93.7%. Churches cannot continue growth over an extended period of time unless people feel well accepted and well cared for within the community of faith, so it is no surprise to see that the percentage in agreement runs so high in those congregations.

The Nature of Hospitality

The word hospitality is not new. We practice it in various ways as part of everyday life. At times, especially with those we already know and trust or know through others, we model it almost perfectly. We speak of southern hospitality and under-stand the meaning of "hospitality rooms" and "hospitality suites."

The word hospitality is often used to describe the entire hotel-motel-restaurant industry; and there are colleges, universities, and specialty schools that use that word to describe what they offer. When we travel, we experience instances of pleasant hospitality in some of the places we stay; and we also experience instances of rudeness. The purpose of the hospitality in these settings is to persuade people to feel good about the money they have spent and to want to return to the same place.

Steve and his wife Sara, like many others, have appreciated the kind of hospitality they have experienced in visiting the Disney theme parks in California and in Florida. On a recent trip to Florida, however, they were disappointed to find:

- A new entrance security system that required a finger-print through an electronic device to be sure that multiple-day tickets didn't get used by someone else. And no one present could explain whether or not any permanent record was kept of the fingerprints. It felt like the park was saying: "Welcome to the Magic Kingdom, and by the way, we want your fingerprint because we don't trust you."

- A hostess at a Narnia exhibit, which was very popular with young children, yelled at people for not standing at the right place for admittance. Then they admitted the people standing patiently at one set of doors and forgot the people standing at another set of doors.

- A hostess at a Nemo ride separated an elderly man who did not speak English from the rest of his party even though there was room for him with the others in his group. Then that hostess let another large party go ahead and board the ride before letting the elderly man proceed. He was upset and clearly did not understand what was happening.

So even the Magic Kingdom has problems with hospitality!

We use the word hospitality to describe persons who exhibit extraordinary graciousness. Being hospitable is for some the opposite of being rude. The word also evokes images of tea parties, pleasant conversations, and an aura of coziness.

The meaning and explanation of hospitality, however, go deeper than those images. The experience and practice of hospitality lies at the very core of what it means to be a Christian. Its roots are woven into the foundation of Judaism and Christianity. An old Hebrew proverb notes that "hospitality to strangers is greater than reverence for the name of God" [Robert E. Meagher in "Stranger at the Gate" in *Parabola 2*].

In the New Testament, the Letter to the Hebrews makes clear the importance of hospitality: "Do not neglect to show hospitality to strangers, for by doing that some have entertained angels without knowing it" [13:2]. In the first three editions of their popular book **Widening the Welcome of Your Church**, Fred Bernhard and Steve Clapp offered the following definitions of hospitality and of the stranger:

> **Hospitality** is the **attitude** and **practice** of providing the **atmosphere** and **opportunities**, however risky, in which strangers are free to become friends, thereby feeling accepted, included, and loved. The relationship thus opens up the possibility for eventual communion among the host, the stranger, and God.

> The **stranger** is any person or group not known to
> the host. The host perceives that this unknown
> person or group has the potential for relationship
> as an enemy or as a friend.

In their book *Hospitality: Life in a Time of Fear* and in the
newest edition of *Widening the Welcome of Your Church*, they
offered an additional definition:

> **Hospitality** involves recognizing the presence of
> Christ in family, friends, coworkers, neighbors,
> and complete strangers. It means responding to
> others as we would respond to the presence of
> Christ in our midst.

That definition has become the one that we like the most
because it emphasizes the fact that hospitality needs to be
extended not only to guests, to strangers, but to all those with
whom we interact in the church and in other settings.

Hospitality is not something optional for the church. It is in
fact the very essence of the church's life and witness. As you
learn to improve your practice of hospitality, you will find
relationships transformed not only with the stranger but also with
those in the body of Christ you already know and with your
friends and family. Being the church means learning how to
practice the biblical art of hospitality, to recognize the presence
of Christ in others, and to build transforming relationships.

The obligation to hospitality and the opportunity to be
enriched by hospitality do not end when someone officially joins
the membership of the congregation! It's part of how we relate to
one another all the time. That hospitality must be deep, standing
at the very core of who we are as Christian people, and it also

must be wide, reaching out to all those with whom we are connected.

In this book we hope to give you information, motivation, and strategies that will enable you to deepen your own hospitality and to deepen the hospitality of those within your congregation. A deep and wide hospitality can transform the life of the congregation. We hope you will not only read this book yourself but also that you will ask others to read it and that you will consider having a congregation-wide study of it.

When searching for a title for this book, we considered the possibility of a title like "Hospitality and Assimilation" because part of what we are endeavoring to do is to help individuals and congregations more thoroughly assimilate new people. But even the use of the word assimilation implies that there is some point after which people are fully a part of the church and the obligation to hospitality is no longer present. That is not true.

The need for hospitality continues in the church and in our own lives as Christian people because it applies to all of our relationships. Our friend and colleague Joan Hershey wrote a booklet that is a guide to hospitality for greeters and ushers that carried the creative title *The First Thirty Seconds*. Certainly we make (or fail to make) an impression on people within the first few seconds of meeting them, and the emphasis of that booklet is important. But hospitality needs to be extended not only to those we have known for only thirty seconds but also to those we have known for thirty days, for three years, and for thirty years.

Here are a few other points about hospitality that we want to make as you begin the adventure of this study with us:

1. Hospitality is not itself a strategy for church growth; but if you truly learn how to practice it, your church will

grow. A congregation that practices biblical hospitality will be filled with passion and vitality and will develop a caring, inviting personality. Your own life will be enriched as well with new friendships, the joy of more energy in the congregation, and a closer relationship with Christ. People will be pulled toward you and toward your congregation. When members of a church start becoming excited about hospitality, others want to be part of it.

2. Hospitality will not succeed over the long run in your church if it is simply another "program" that you do. Hospitality needs to be part of the DNA of the congregation, part of the core of the identity of the church. We are seeking with hospitality to treat others as we want to be treated, to truly be living out the Golden Rule in our lives and in the life of the church.

3. Hospitality means getting rid of distinctions between "insiders" and "outsiders." Think about the distinctions:

- Between those who are visitors and those who are members.

- Between those who grew up in the denomination and those who did not.

- Between those who are related to other persons in the church family and those who are not.

- Between those who have belonged to the congregation for decades and those who have been around for only a few months or years.

"Outsiders" have to become "insiders" if people are to feel the kind of connection that makes them want to continue as part of the faith community. Even our motivation for seeking new people for the life of the church needs to be examined. If we are primarily seeking new people because we need more volunteers for the church's programs and because we need more financial giving to keep the church strong, we are doing our outreach for the wrong reasons. Sharing the faith with others and bringing others into the life of the church should be at the core of what we are about as Christian people. If we continue thinking of insiders and outsiders, others will feel that and will drift away. We'll have much more to say about insiders and outsiders as this book progresses.

The assimilation of people starts when people first have contact with the church, but it continues for as long as people are connected. We have to demonstrate to those who are initially outsiders that there is a place for them in the life of the church. As people visit and begin involvement in a congregation, one of their core questions is: "Is there a place for me here?"

Fred Bernhard knows of a large family that has an unusual tradition at their annual reunion. A couple of people will invite a "mystery guest" to the reunion and ask that person to become part of the family. Fred has had the experience of being that mystery guest and of being grafted into a family to which he is not related genetically. In a very real sense, the church as the family of God is continually at work grafting in new people.

4. None of this is an argument against having clearly articulated core beliefs as a congregation. It's very important to be clear about the core beliefs of the congregation, and it's also true that not every single person is the right fit for a particular congregation. The more clear we are about our core beliefs and the better we articulate them, the more readily those who are guests can discern whether or not the congregation is the right fit for them. We should show hospitality to everyone, but we should also respect the fact that some people will determine that a different congregation is a better fit for them. That is not a negative reflection on us or on them.

5. Much of what passes as "church growth" in North America today really consists of nothing more than people changing pews. Someone who has been dissatisfied in one congregation decides to become part of another congregation. That decision sometimes results in that person having a greater level of activity and commitment, so in some instances it may be the best decision. But that really does not represent growth in the kingdom of God.

We need to find the ways to reach out to people who are not part of the church community, including those who may have been hurt by something that happened to them in a church in the past. To do that, and to avoid hurting people in the future, we need a hospitality that is truly deep and wide. It needs to be a hospitality which penetrates deeply—to the core of who we are as individuals and as a congregation. And it needs to be a very wide hospitality that seeks to embrace all who claim Jesus as Lord.

Chapter Two
A Biblical Look
at Assimilation and Hospitality

Acts 2:42–47

Concept: The Bible affirms that hospitality is an obligation and that *all* people should be assimilated into the life of the church.

Blake and Marcia had been members of St. Luke's Church for ten years. During those years, they had grown in their commitment to both Christ and the church. They were regular in attendance, they were involved in leadership, and they had significantly increased their financial giving. Then a downsizing in the company for which Blake worked pushed him out of his high-paying position near the start of the year. He and Marcia kept thinking he would find another good job soon, so they didn't make any significant adjustments in their lifestyles. They did get behind on their church pledge, but they thought they could easily make that up later in the year when Blake had a better job. The better job, unfortunately, didn't come. They ended the year having paid $1,400 on a $5,000 pledge.

Their church ended the year financially in the red. During announcements at worship in the following January, the Finance Chairperson called attention to the fact that there were over $20,000 in unpaid pledges that were the major reason for the church being in the red. Blake and Marcia were overwhelmed with guilt, and they stopped coming to church.

After they had been absent for a couple of months, one of the church's pastors came to visit them. They simply said that they had been very busy with Blake looking for a new job and had gotten out of the habit of coming. They promised to return soon. Neither they nor the pastor said anything about their pledge. Marcia and Blake talked later and thought it was possible that the pastor didn't know that they had failed to meet their pledge. But the Finance Chairperson, the Treasurer, and the Financial Secretary certainly did; and Marcia and Blake couldn't stand the idea of facing them at church. They ended up moving to a new community, but they didn't get involved in another congregation.

Leslie was twenty-eight years old and had just moved across the country for a new job. Following a failed marriage, she had spent the last three years struggling with the issue of her own sexual orientation. She had come to the conclusion that she was lesbian. Though nothing had happened sexually, she had begun going out with a person of the same sex shortly before the move across the country.

The church to which she had belonged before the move was one that had gone on record as being openly welcoming and affirming of persons of gay or lesbian orientation. She had been able to talk openly in that church with her pastor and other members about her struggles. When she moved, she intentionally sought out a church of the same denomination. She felt warmly welcomed the first three times she attended. There had been no reason to tell anyone about her sexual orientation, but the hospitality of the church seemed good to her.

Then came what she would remember for years as "the sermon" in which the pastor of the church condemned homo-sexuality and also condemned the efforts in the denomination to approve ordination for persons of homosexual orientation. Leslie did not return to the church. When a layperson from the con-gregation stopped by to visit with her and to say that she had been missed, Leslie decided to tell the truth. The person visiting with Leslie told her that not everyone in the congregation agreed with the pastor on this issue and that there were at least a couple of people in the congregation who had a homosexual orientation. She encouraged Leslie not to give up on the church; but Leslie said, "How would you feel if the minister preached that your heterosexual orientation was sinful? Would you think that you could just overlook that and keep on coming?"

Bill and Ashley felt very good when they joined First Church and were enthusiastic about what they could contribute to the congregation. People had been very warm to them and were obviously delighted to have their participation. As the months passed, however, they increasingly felt on the outside rather than the inside of the congregation. The majority of the people in the church had been attending there for ten years or more, some for as long as thirty or forty years. Bill and Ashley increasingly felt as though there were inner circles and cliques in the church to which they were never going to belong. The initial welcome had been great, but it became clear to them that they were always going to be on the outside looking into the social groups and the decision-making structure of the congregation.

Insiders and Outsiders

Why begin a chapter on the Bible with three examples of people not feeling fully accepted within a congregation? The reality is that each situation described involves people failing to live out some of the most important teachings of Scripture, including the Great Commandment: "'You shall love the Lord your God with all your heart, and with all your soul, and with all your strength, and with all your mind; and your neighbor as yourself'" [Luke 10:27].

The command to love our neighbors as ourselves is an easy one to say and also an easy one with which to agree, but actually living it out in our daily lives and in the life of the church can be a more difficult process.

The way that a church handles finances can have a significant impact on the lives of its members. It's of course important for people to be helped to see that all of our possessions come to us from God and that we should be sharing generously with the church and with other charitable needs as an outgrowth of our faith. But the reality is that life situations change. Churches that are sensitive to that reality have a statement on their pledge forms and on their regular financial statements which says the pledge can be changed at any time by contacting the treasurer or financial secretary. Steve Clapp, who has done considerable research on stewardship and the spiritual life, encourages churches to use the words "intention of giving" rather than "pledge" because of the less legalistic tone.

At least four things would have been different if Blake, Marcia, and their church had followed seriously the admonition to love our neighbors as ourselves. First, the church would have had information on changing a pledge on statements so people would know that was possible. Second, when their giving got so far behind, one of the people connected with finance in the church would have contacted them to ask if they needed to modify the pledge. Third, Marcia and Blake themselves would have recognized that the church needed to know they could not meet the pledge and would have said something about it to the treasurer or financial secretary. Fourth, when they still did not return to church after the pastor's visit, someone else would have made a contact and endeavored to discover what the problem was.

What about the situation for Leslie? The issue of homosexuality in the church is a complex one, and opinions are divided on this topic in many congregations and denominations. Some point to biblical passages that appear to condemn the practice of homosexuality. Others point to the Genesis passages on the goodness of creation and current scientific evidence that indicates sexual orientation may not really be a "choice" for large numbers of people. If creation is good and some people simply have a sexual orientation different than that of others, then there is good reason to consider the possibility that homosexuality is a part of God's diversity.

We are left with a relatively small number of passages that question the practice of homosexual behavior in contrast to the enormous number of passages that emphasize the goodness of creation and the importance of loving others. Many scholars put the small number of condemnatory passages into a more careful historical context and conclude that these passages were all speaking to specific issues of the time and that the prohibitions should not necessarily be generalized to people today. Old Testament Scriptures tell us to stone disobedient children, but we fortunately do not follow that counsel today!

A full discussion of the topic of homosexuality goes beyond the scope of what we can accomplish in this book, but it would be unrealistic for us to ignore the issue. The reality is that a significant number of persons in our society do have a nonheterosexual orientation, and churches must decide how to respond to them. Christian Community's national study [published in the book *Faith Matters: Teenagers, Religion, and Sexuality*] revealed that about ten percent of teens in the average congregation have a homosexual orientation, a bisexual orientation, or are struggling to determine what their orientation really is. Do similar percentages apply to adults in our congregations? We are not aware of any current data that would answer that question. Most teens

31

who are not heterosexual choose to be relatively quiet in the church about their orientation; adults may well be the same, especially if the church has a harsh attitude toward homosexuality.

Obviously Leslie's denomination is not of one mind on this issue when the acceptance in the earlier congregation is contrasted with the condemnation in the one she was visiting. But given the divided opinions on this topic, one has to wonder if a strong attack on homosexuality from the pulpit is the best way to approach this issue. How many people are there in the congregation who, perhaps unknown to the pastor, have a non-heterosexual orientation? Leslie may well be in the wrong congregation for her, but the approach could have been kinder and could have recognized the reality of other points of view on the topic. Again, we need to consider the question of what the loving thing to do really is.

In fact the authors of this book are not themselves of one mind on every aspect of the topic of homosexuality, though all three agree on the importance of warm hospitality to all people regardless of sexual orientation or gender. One of the authors belongs to a denomination that has an official position of being welcoming to gay and lesbian people but of not condoning what is referred to as the homosexual lifestyle. Two of the authors belong to a denomination that actually had a moratorium on talking about the issue of sexual orientation because the topic caused so much tension in the denomination. One of the authors has directed a study on strategies to increase the unconditional acceptance and involvement of lesbian, gay, bisexual, and transgender (LGBT) people in the life of the church. All three recognize that local congregations and denominations are in a time of discernment as they endeavor through prayer, study, and discussion to determine the right ways to respond on this issue.

Bill and Ashley are the victims of what is probably the most common problem with hospitality and assimilation in many churches today. People have learned how to give a warm initial welcome, perhaps how to take cookies or bread to visitors, and how to initially pull people into the life of the church. But the reality is that the friendship circles of many of our churches are not really open to new people. Those like Bill and Ashley discover in time that they really are outsiders wanting to be on the inside.

If we really cared about outsiders, we would model the apostolic church. Look at the first and second chapters of Acts:

- People prayed continually.

- People grew in the faith.

- People made commitments to Christ and the Christian community.

- People acted on their faith.

Here's a description in Acts 2:44–47:

> *All who believed were together and had all things in common; they would sell their possessions and goods and distribute the proceeds to all, as any had need. Day by day, as they spent much time together in the temple, they broke bread from house to house and ate their food with glad and generous hearts, praising God and having the goodwill of all the people. And day by day the Lord added to their number those who were being saved.*

There were not insiders and outsiders. The level of commitment was so high that people sold their possessions and also spent great amounts of time together. They saw the new people who came to them as being sent by God. In *The Message*'s treatment of those verses, Peterson says it like this:

People in general liked what they saw.

We like the image of Jesus calling us to be "fishers of men" or in more contemporary translations, "fishers of people." This image grows out of Jesus calling Simon and his brother Andrew as disciples as they were casting their net into the sea. "And Jesus said to them, 'Follow me, and I will make you fish for people.'" The problem, Fred Bernhard frequently points out in his popular seminars and workshops on hospitality, is that too many of us do selective fishing. We're either not casting the net, or we pick out the ones we want rather than taking the whole net to the shore.

That's what happened in all three of the opening examples of this chapter. Blake and Marcia were not helped to stay in the net when they were in a time of great difficulty. The pastor preparing his sermon did not think about the possibility of people like Leslie being in the congregation. And the long-time members of the church Bill and Ashley joined were too focused on one another to truly integrate the two of them into the friendship circles of the church.

Hospitality in the Orient

In biblical times, people who traveled were not able to make reservations at a Hilton, Sheraton, Embassy Suites, Red Roof Inn, or Residence Inn. They didn't have chain restaurants available everywhere they traveled. A journey across the desert was a dangerous and often unpleasant endeavor.

People throughout the Mediterranean world regarded the provision of food, lodging, and protection as a virtue and sacred
duty. The survival of travelers could depend on that hospitality.
The following were components in the ritual of hospitality as it
was commonly practiced:

- **Bowing:** In receiving a desert guest, the host would
  often bend at the knees and gradually lower his or her
  body until touching the ground. This act revealed the
  host's desire to render the highest possible honor to
  the stranger-guest.

- **Feet-washing:** People wore sandals, and a day on the
  desert meant dirty, hot, and often sore feet. Washing
  the feet was an act of kindness which conveyed honor
  to the guest.

- **Preparing and serving food:** The host might devote
  considerable time and expense to preparing food for
  the guest. The generous Bedouins were known to
  deny themselves for the sake of the guest. The host's
  family ate later from what remained. The thoughtful
  guest always left a portion of food on the dish.

- **Needs of animals:** The host also provided the needed
  food and lodging for the camels of the guest.

- **All guests were seen as potential friends:** Obviously
  the stranger can represent a friend or an enemy, but
  the starting assumption in the Ancient Near East was
  that the stranger was a potential friend. Names were
  not exchanged until after the meal was eaten, if at all.
  An exchange of names and background information
  was not considered a requirement for hospitality.

Those who have read *Widening the Welcome of Your Church* by Fred Bernhard and Steve Clapp may be familiar with these practices, but we share them again here because of their importance for us in looking at assimilation as well as hospitality. We no longer face the same kind of dangers and hardships in our travels, but the need to show and to receive hospitality continues to be just as important in our time.

The stranger could also expect protection from the host. If a stranger was being pursued by an enemy, the fleeing person only had to touch the peg of the host's tent to be safe. The pursuer would be forced to peer helplessly from outside the tent while the guest was entertained. That protection generally extended for thirty-six hours, the period thought to be sustained by a meal or the time needed for salt to leave the stomach. That length of time permitted a head start for the fugitive. Psalm 23 takes on new meaning when one thinks about the tradition of hospitality in relationship to these words:

> *You prepare a table before me*
> *in the presence of my enemies;*
> *you anoint my head with oil;*
> *my cup overflows.*

Abraham and Hospitality

Genesis 18:1–15 describes the hospitality of Abraham toward three men who appeared near the entrance to his tent. Biblical scholars (including Vawter, Von Rad, and Fretheim) agree that the three strangers are personages of Yahweh, though we are not clear in precisely what way. In *The New Interpreter's Bible*, Terence Fretheim offers this perspective: "From the narrator's point of view, Yahweh appears to Abraham at his home (v.1). From Abraham's point of view, however, three men stand near

36

him (v.2). Yahweh has assumed human form appearing among the three men; the other two are angelic attendants" [Vol. I, p. 462–463]. Consider the text:

> *The Lord appeared to Abraham by the oaks of*
> *Mamre, as he sat at the entrance of his tent in the*
> *heat of the day. He looked up and saw three men*
> *standing near him. When he saw them, he ran*
> *from the tent entrance to meet them, and bowed*
> *down to the ground. He said, "My lord, if I find*
> *favor with you, do not pass by your servant. Let a*
> *little water be brought, and wash your feet, and*
> *rest yourselves under the tree. Let me bring a*
> *little bread, that you may refresh yourselves, and*
> *after that you may pass on—since you have come*
> *to your servant."*
> *So they said, "Do as you have said." And*
> *Abraham hastened into the tent to Sarah, and said,*
> *"Make ready quickly three measures of choice*
> *flour, knead it, and make cakes." Abraham ran to*
> *the herd, and took a calf, tender and good, and*
> *gave it to the servant, who hastened to prepare it.*
> *Then he took curds and milk and the calf that he*
> *had prepared, and set it before them; and he stood*
> *by them under the tree while they ate.*
>
> **Genesis 18:1–8**

Abraham offers hospitality without being aware of the divine presence. That hospitality is consistent with the practice in the Ancient Near East and includes these elements:

- Abraham bows to them.

- Abraham offers them water, rest, and food.

- They accept.

- The meal is prepared and includes a calf, which would have been reserved for a special occasion, and butter, which was greatly prized by the nomad.

- Abraham waits on them while they eat.

- The strangers did not reveal their identity nor did they offer any gift or payment prior to the meal.

In sharing the calf and the butter, Abraham and Sarah gave far more than custom required. They chose to treat the three men as honored guests, and they did so without expecting anything in return. In verses 9–15, one of them tells Sarah that she will have a son. The fact that the gift of a child was promised can be seen as a response to their hospitality, but the promise of a son had already been made in the preceding chapter. The hospitality existed for its own sake, and Abraham has been lifted up as a model because of it. Had Abraham and Sarah refused hospitality to the strangers, they would have shut themselves off from the blessings God intended—not just the blessing of a son but also the blessing of God's presence.

Jesus and Hospitality

In the New Testament, we find the practice of hospitality directly linked to its practice in Judaism. As in the Old Testament passages, the New Testament accounts do not focus the issue on the worthiness of the stranger but rather on the faithfulness of the one from whom hospitality is sought. Several passages give helpful perspectives to us:

- **Matthew 26:6–13** gives an account of Jesus in the home of Simon the leper. Going to the home of a leper would have been unacceptable to the religious establishment, but Jesus does so without hesitation. While he is there, a woman pours a costly ointment on his head, showing a hospitality which foreshadows his burial.

How readily do we reach out to, warmly welcome, and integrate into our congregations those who have AIDS, those who have significant physical limitations, and those with mental or emotional challenges in their lives?

- **Luke 10:29–37** tells the Parable of the Good Samaritan. This well known parable answers the important question: "Who is my neighbor?" The parable strongly reinforces that all people are our neighbors, and the obligation to care for others cuts across all religious, ethnic, and economic lines.

How readily do we see all people as our neighbors? The hero of this parable was a Samaritan, a person looked down upon by many who would have first heard these words. Who are the outsiders for the church today? And who are the people inside the church who are made to feel like outsiders?

- **Luke 14:12–24** includes the Parable of the Great Dinner, in which Jesus advocates that the one who extends hospitality invite "the poor, the crippled, the lame, and the blind. And you will be blessed, because they cannot repay you, for you will be repaid at the resurrection of the righteous" [v.13–14].

What would it mean for our often affluent churches if we truly integrated persons who, because of problems in their lives, have low incomes? How many of our churches are prepared to deal with significant economic diversity?

- **Luke 19:1–10** shows Jesus again with one of the people the religious authorities would have avoided — this time with Zacchaeus the tax collector. A similar reference is found in **Luke 5:27–32** in which Jesus eats with "a large crowd of tax collectors" [v.29].

Are the wealthy and influential outsiders to our churches? Are those of us in congregations predominately composed of low-income or middle-income households prepared to extend true hospitality to persons of wealth and influence? Does it even occur to us to invite those persons into participation in our congregations?

- **John 13:1–20** describes Jesus' washing the feet of the disciples at the time of the Last Supper. Jesus not only accepted the hospitality of others, but he also displayed hospitality through his entire ministry. The ritual or ordinance of washing the feet of another goes back to the custom in the Ancient Near East and is a clear affirmation of the value put on the one who is the guest.

Some churches continue to practice the ritual of foot-washing as a part of a Love Feast or Holy Communion (or the Eucharist, depending on the language of your tradition). But Jesus is describing here not just an outward act but an inward attitude to be lived out in our relationships as part of the Christian community. Are we prepared to truly love all people who come to our churches enough to wash their feet?

The Least of These

Matthew 25:31–46 presents an account very similar in some ways to that in Genesis 18, studied earlier. We are told to reach out to those who are hungry, naked, homeless, or imprisoned. When we show hospitality to such persons, it is as though the kindness was actually being shown to Christ:

> *"Lord, when was it that we saw you hungry or thirsty or a stranger or naked or sick or in prison, and did not take care of you?"*
>
> *Then he will answer them, "Truly I tell you, just as you did not do it to one of the least of these, you did not do it to me"* [v.45–46].

In this passage, Jesus makes it clear that we are not to reject the needy stranger like the son of man who was rejected and crucified. The stranger is to be welcomed, accepted, fed, and clothed. Welcoming the stranger opens the door to building relationships and developing deeper communion with one another and with God.

But this is not just an encouragement to reach out to the least of those outside our congregations. The words should guide our relationships as well with those already in our congregations. If we truly recognize the presence of Christ in others, then our relationships with them are going to be transformed. It's not only a matter of reaching out to people in society we might otherwise ignore, but it's also a matter of continuing to treat with great kindness all those who are in the congregation.

We need to apply these words not only to persons with physical needs but also to those with spiritual needs. Some of us who may do well relating to someone with less income than we have may find ourselves having more difficulty relating to those in the Christian community who have strong personalities, who haven't learned how to get along well with others, who make us feel uncomfortable because of having a different sexual orientation, and so the list could be continued. Recognizing the presence of Christ in others can truly change how we feel about them and how we relate to them. The same principle of hospitality gets reinforced in these additional New Testament passages:

- **Matthew 10:40–42** points out that those who welcome the disciples of Christ are in fact welcoming Christ himself. The passage goes on to say that "'whoever gives even a cup of cold water to one of these little ones in the name of a disciple—truly I tell you, none of these will lose their reward.'"

- **1 Peter 4:7–11** urges us to show love in all our relationships and to give evidence of hospitality. We are to "be hospitable to one another without complaining" [v.9].

- **Hebrews 13:1–2** encourages us to show "hospitality to strangers, for by doing that some have entertained angels without knowing it."

Whether we think of encountering an angel in the stranger, as suggested in Hebrew 13, or the actual presence of Christ, as suggested in Matthew 25, there is no question about the importance placed on hospitality to the stranger.

Deepening Community

The Bible urges the broad practice of hospitality, the recognition of Christ in all those we encounter. It also makes it clear that real hospitality isn't just a matter of initial friendship to bring people into the life of our congregations. True hospitality is something that we make part of our daily lives and also part of daily life in the church community.

In Peterson's translation of **Romans 15:7–13** [*The Message*], we read about insiders and outsiders. The outsiders were the Gentiles, and the insiders were the Jews. Jesus sought to bring the insiders and the outsiders together. The words of Romans 15:12 are related to Psalm 18:49 and Isaiah 11:10. "The root of Jesse shall come, the one who rises to rule the Gentiles; in him the Gentiles shall hope."

In **Ephesians 4:11–16**, we are reminded that people have different gifts but that all of us together compose the body of Christ. "[S]peaking the truth in love, we must grow up in every way into him who is the head, into Christ, from whom the whole body, joined and knit together by every ligament with which it is equipped, as each part is working properly, promotes the body's growth in building itself up in love" [v. 15–16]. The church as the body of Christ needs the contributions of everyone—including Blake and Marcia, Leslie, and Bill and Ashley.

The issues of hospitality and assimilation not only apply to new members of the congregation but to those who have been part of the church for decades. One of the authors of this book recently visited with a Sunday school class composed primarily of persons who had been members of a congregation for thirty years or more, some for as long as sixty-five years. The church to which they belonged was growing rapidly, and most of the new members were young adults. Members of this class of long-time members shared their anxiety about being forgotten or marginalized by the church in the midst of efforts to reach new people. True assimilation means not just helping newer people feel welcome but also integrating them into the full life of the congregation and building connections with those who have been in the church for decades. Older members should not be made to feel on the outside because the church is growing and changing.

As this book continues, we want to explore pragmatically how we can deepen and widen the hospitality of the church so that we not only reach out to all people but also integrate them thoroughly into the life of our congregations. That means developing a continuing concern for one another, regardless of the length of time we have been part of a congregation.

Chapter Three
The DNA of the Inclusive Church

Romans 15:1–13

Concept: The congregation that takes biblical hospitality seriously has a different DNA, a different core identity than other congregations. Long-time members take the initiative by reaching out to guests and by helping them become incorporated into the congregation.

Adam was excited by his first Sunday at Lakeside Church. It was a much larger congregation than his hometown church, which made him a little apprehensive; but it also seemed to be an exciting congregation. The music was uplifting, and the sermon was inspiring.

Having enjoyed the Sunday morning experience so much, Adam returned to the church on Sunday evening for the TwentyThirtySomething Group. He'd picked up information about this group at the Hospitality Table that morning. A young adult woman named Tabitha, about his age, had noticed him reading the material. She'd introduced herself; told him about the group, which was primarily social; and invited him to come.

About a hundred young adults, apparently all single, gathered in the fellowship hall for the start of the evening. This was about the same size as Adam's home congregation, and it was a high-energy group. Tabitha turned out to be one of the leaders, along with Pastor Rick. The group spent about ten minutes singing, had a very short devotional from Rick, and then received instructions for a Driving Scavenger Hunt.

People divided into teams that would drive around the city together to take digital pictures of people, places, and things that met the criteria on the Driving Scavenger Hunt list. Most of the teams had four persons, but a few had five.

Adam had initially hoped that he might be on the same team as Tabitha, but it turned out that she and Rick had designed the hunt and weren't actually going on it themselves. Adam found himself with four others, two men and two women. All four obviously knew each other well, but they initially made a strong effort to include Adam.

As the hunt progressed, however, Adam increasingly felt like a fifth wheel. Not only did the others know each other well, but it actually turned out that he was with two couples who had been dating for awhile. He felt especially awkward in the back seat by Alyssa and Kent who had their hands all over each other as the evening progressed.

He also found it hard to contribute to the group because he just wasn't that familiar with the city. He felt good a couple of times when he made suggestions that proved helpful, but most of the clues made no sense to him.

When they returned to the church and went into the fellowship hall again, the two couples went in separate directions without any effort to invite Adam to sit with them. As he sat down by a couple of other people, Adam realized that no one in the car had even asked him where he was working or where he had lived before moving there.

Prizes were awarded to the winners of the hunt, and then the group broke for pizza, soda, and brownies. Adam stood around holding a plate and a can of soda for awhile, unsure of where to sit, until Tabitha came up to him and invited him to the table where she and Rick were sitting with three other people. Both of them did a good job including him in the conversation for a while. Then the two of them started circulating to greet people at other tables, and Adam found himself feeling pretty excluded from the conversation of the other three at the table. He gulped down his brownie and left.

Adam's conclusion was that Tabitha and Rick were pretty good at reaching out to new people and helping them feel included but that the members of the group didn't have the same concern for inclusion. He went home sorry that he'd come; the sense of being on the fringe of the group deepened the loneliness he was already feeling in the new city.

Darrell had attended a large, highly liturgical congregation as a child but had become completely inactive during his youth and young adult years, when he had experimented with many things but not with church. A few years later, with his wife Beth and two children, he decided it was time to try church again. They went as a family to a different congregation and were impressed by the vibrant, everyday faith of the people there. People in the church seemed characterized by strong family life, solid work ethic, and commitment to peace and justice concerns.

"At first all was great," Darrell shared. "It was everything we had hoped for. But as time went on we became aware that we were being treated differently, sometimes being introduced as 'the community people who attend our church,' despite the fact that we had become members."

There were deeper problems in their new church home than Darrell or his family had realized. The church had a split, which left Darrell, Beth, and their children disillusioned. They began attending another congregation but found it a more difficult fit. Although not entirely comfortable, they kept participating because, as Darrell explained it, "the theology was in sync with what we believed, and the people cooked such fantastic food!"

One day the pastor asked, "When will you become a member?" Darrell replied, "I'm not sure." The pastor forcefully said, "Well, either become a member or leave the church." Under the threat of that blunt ultimatum, Darrell and Beth did join the church. But the pastor's demand was a foretaste of worse things to come. The social fabric of the congregation simply was not open to Darrell, Beth, or even their children; and the pastor was not the only one capable of sharing harsh words. Finally, deeply hurt and disillusioned, they left the church.

The newcomer, the long-time member, the strong, the weak, the rich, the poor, the extravert, the introvert—all are accepted graciously and with love by God. Paul, writing to the first-century Romans, gave encouragement to this new community of faith. "Welcome one another," Paul exclaims, "just as Christ welcomed you, for the glory of God" [v. 15:7]. Through the power and grace of Jesus, it becomes natural to socialize with those outside our normal socioeconomic group and with those who may seem different from us in other ways as well. We are called to include and assimilate within the family of God whomever God sends. Adam, Darrell, and Beth did not experience that inclusion in their church experiences.

Our Self-Perception

Often long-time congregational members take for granted the church's friendliness, its inclusiveness, its family atmosphere. When they think of their fellowship, they feel good about the strength of their relationships in the church and remember times others have been there to help them with the problems in their lives. Long-time members feel accepted and assume that others feel the same way. The congregation, to them, radiates an at-home feeling, and everyone feels comfortable. But what about the "outsider" who just came for the second Sunday, or the stranger who is not dressed like everyone else? What about the person who has not found friends in the church after three months?

When we have guests in our homes, an attitude of healthy hospitality causes us to ask, "How can we make you feel comfortable? How can we make you feel at home here? How can we get to know each other better?" Does that happen in the church? We may feel our church exudes inclusiveness. But how does it look and feel to the newcomer? If we want to establish an hospitable church, it is important to discover what guests experience and think as well as what members experience and think.

Many of our congregations need to evaluate our attitudes regarding new people. Do we really want new persons to sit in our pews, to take the time of our pastor, and to bring new challenges? Ed Bontrager had contact with a church that was being quite successful in reaching out to new people. The attendance was growing, and many people were becoming involved in the congregation. And then a distressed long-time member asked with some hostility, "Where are you getting all these people?" The speaker was definitely not happy about so many new people intruding into the life of the church and bringing change with them.

A church that is going to grow generally finds that it is necessary to put a little greater emphasis on the needs of new people than on the needs of long-time members. As Fred Bernhard shares in his workshops, "Do a little something more for the guest. Give the priority to the guest, just as you would in your home."

In congregational studies, Christian Community often asks members on surveys to indicate their agreement with this statement: "Our pastor(s) should spend as much time in ministry to unchurched people as to people in our church." Across North

America, an average of 23.8% of the active members surveyed agree with that statement. In congregations that are growing, however, 65.4% agree with the statement. Growing congregations agree that the pastor should give priority to outreach, and they are also more likely to reflect positive hospitality to those who are new to the church.

The challenge of giving special care to those who are new to the church affects congregations of every size:

- In small congregations, the task of assimilation can theoretically be easier than in larger congregations because there are fewer people with whom to become connected. In healthy small congregations, this really is the case. In some, however, a visitor may feel that he or she has intruded into someone else's family reunion!

- The social networks in medium-sized congregations are often more open than in smaller congregations, and this can be a real plus to the assimilation process. In a medium-sized congregation, however, it begins to become easy for everyone to assume that connecting with a new person is someone else's job.

- Large congregations can seem overwhelming to visitors for whom personal connections are important, but they also offer a degree of anonymity that can be attractive for some new people. Over a period of time, however, most people do not want to remain anonymous but want in fact to become part of some of the social networks of the church. Large churches can do an excellent job at assimilation, but it is very important to have carefully structured small group programs and to intentionally see that new people become part of smaller settings as well as large ones.

As a local church pastor for many years, Ed Bontrager noticed that God didn't have trouble sending new people to the church, but that the church did at times have trouble accepting those new people and folding them into circles of fellowship. Reaching new people through evangelistic outreach can get them to visit the church, to give attendance a try, but people will not continue coming unless the church's DNA really is inclusive, unless the church as a whole really does want new people and care about their feeling included.

The following chart shows some of the important differences between new members and longer-time members of the church. While there are certainly significant exceptions to these short descriptions, the overall characteristics tend to be true and can be helpful in thinking about the different perspectives of these groups of people.

New Members and Long-Time Members

Some Important Differences

NEW MEMBERS	LONG-TIME MEMBERS
1. Join in large part because of personal needs being met.	1. Continue as members in large part because of meaningful relationships in the congregation.
2. Tend to be enthusiastic about the congregation.	2. May be less enthusiastic because of disillusioning experiences or because they have come to take the church more for granted.
3. Are likely to invite others to come to church.	3. Are less likely to think of inviting others to church.

4. Feel like outsiders part of the time and don't yet have a strong sense of belonging.	4. Feel assimilated and have a strong sense of belonging.
5. Are generally future-oriented.	5. Are more likely to be focused on the past more than the future.
6. Are likely not to know a great deal about the denomination to which the church belongs and not to have high loyalty to the denomination.	6. Are likely to know more about the denomination to which the church belongs and to have more loyalty to the denomination.
7. Are interested in change and innovation in the church.	7. Are more concerned with maintaining the status quo.
8. Have a strong attachment to the current staff of the church.	8. May have a stronger attachment to past staff members of the church who have helped them through difficult times.
9. Are not strongly attached to the current physical facilities.	9. May consider the facility and its contents sacred.
10. Are more likely to leave the church if their needs are not met—or to simply stop coming.	10. Are not as likely to leave the church because they have stronger loyalty to the congregation and more relationships with people.

The concept for the preceding chart is based on one from the Institute for American Church Growth but the content has been significantly changed.

Is the Church Velcro or Teflon?

Some church growth experts have been using the imagery of "Velcro" and "Teflon" to refer to churches and their assimilation capacity. Churches that are Velcro do all they can to help people stick once they come. On the other hand, Teflon churches are generally not growth-oriented, and do not have systems in place to keep new people, so consequently, they slide off the edges very easily.

Hospitality serves as the primary key in assisting new people to stick. While initial hospitality has a lot to do with people deciding to join a congregation, long-term hospitality is what determines whether or not people stay. In an era when many of us feel that time is our scarcest resource, hospitality falters. "In a fast-food culture," a wise Benedictine monk observes, "you have to remind yourself that some things cannot be done quickly. Hospitality takes time." It isn't enough to give a warm welcome when people first attend. Intentional efforts must be made to graft new people into the total life of the congregation.

True hospitality results in the social networks of the congregation being open and in new members being able to form friendships with long-time members and with other new members. If those relationships do not begin to form, most people will not continue coming to church.

Velcro for the long-term members sometimes turns out to be Teflon for the new people. The glue which gives the church a sense of direction and identity such as a common history, social class, family ties, the building, a common theology, and certain musical tastes are all the same factors that can cause some newcomers to feel excluded. In fact, the stronger the inclusive factors, the more difficult it may be for new people. A wise person said, "Justification is by faith, but assimilation is by works!" It takes planning and effort to truly integrate persons who have no relatives or long-term friends in the church, come from another denomination, and are in the dark with respect to historical significant events in the church.

Congregations, however, can change! Change is possible both for newly established congregations and for those with very long histories. It's a matter of intentionality and of learning to think about the issues involved in being a truly welcoming congregation. Your study of this book is an important step in that process.

Evangelism and Assimilation

People in some congregations have grown uncomfortable with the word "evangelism." They don't like to think of themselves as "selling" the church or the Christian faith, and they don't want to make others uncomfortable. The reality, however, is that sharing our faith with others is an important part of what God calls us to do. The fact that you are reading this book almost certainly means that your own relationship with Christ has transformed your life in positive ways and that your involvement in the church continues to enrich your life. Those experiences are ones that we should wish for other people.

Evangelism, reaching out to those outside the faith or outside the church, needs to be at the heart of what the church is about. Assimilation is not an issue if we don't have new people coming to our churches!

There is a strong misconception in many Christian churches: that is the conviction that people outside of the church do not believe in God and lack a meaningful faith. The truth is that the majority of persons outside the institutional church in North America in fact do believe in God, even though they may not express that in the same words as those who are active in a local congregation. Certainly there are, or should be, many new people who come to our churches who already have a strong faith in Christ:

- There are persons who were active in a congregation in another community who are potential members because they have moved and need a new church home. This can include people from our own denominational heritage and can also include people from other traditions.

- There are persons who have been hurt in another church. Ed Bontrager knows of a congregation that received 40 new people because of a split in a neighboring church that left people hurt and disillusioned. People who come from such a situation will be looking carefully at how they and others are treated in a new congregation. It's very important for them to feel safe.

- There are people of faith many of us know who have become completely inactive in any congregation. This can include people who simply got out of the habit of regular attendance and people who have become uncomfortable with the church as an institution. They may respond positively to invitations to involvement if they know how important the church is to our own lives.

Sometimes those persons find their way to us without any significant initiative on our part. Most of the time, however, they come because they have been invited by someone who is already part of the church.

There are a growing number of persons in this country who belong to what some call "the church of the bagel or donut and the Sunday newspaper." These are people who have faith in God and may well believe in Christ but who simply do not see the institutional church as a place where that faith will be nurtured. Some of them may have had bad experiences in the church as a child, but many of them have had very few connections with any congregation except for attending the occasional wedding or funeral. These are persons we can reach as well, but it takes a little more effort to convince them of what involvement in the body of Christ can do for them—and of what they can do for others through the church.

Of course there are people who do not embrace the Christian faith and who may feel overtly hostile toward organized religion. Mass evangelism rallies and televised religion certainly reach some new people with the message of Christ, but the majority of people come to the faith through involvement with other Christians and with a local congregation. Persons without any belief in God and with some hostility toward organized religion are not likely to be reached through mass evangelism. They are far more likely to be reached through people like those reading this book!

Evangelism, hospitality, and assimilation are in fact all part of the same continuum of caring about others in the name of Christ:

- **Evangelism** motivates our outreach to people who are not in the church and who may or may not embrace the Christian faith. We reach out to them and seek to bring them into the life of the church and into a deeper faith.

- **Hospitality** is the way we embrace those who visit our congregations *and* those who have been part of our congregations for years. We work to have open social networks in the church, to pull new people into relationships with those who have been in the church for years, and to meet the needs of everyone in the faith community. Hospitality is not just another program of the church but in fact is an attitude and practice that permeates everything that happens in the congregation.

- **Assimilation** is the process by which guests and new members become thoroughly integrated in the total life of the church. It's also the process by which we work to be sure that all members, including long-term ones, feel valued and included.

Ed Bontrager has been especially impressed at the close relationships of evangelism, hospitality, and assimilation at Abundant Life Church in Sarasota, Florida. The senior pastor there provides opportunity each Sunday for some type of mental assent and physical response to the message. It may be as simple as an invitation to come forward for prayer. This is a contemporary variation on the old-fashioned altar call. While this approach isn't a comfortable one for every faith tradition, it has worked very well at the Abundant Life Church. It's not unusual for one or more persons each week at Abundant Life to decide to accept Christ for the first time. This, along with warm hospitality and an effective assimilation system, has helped the church grow from 60 people to an attendance of 500 in just seven years. This model is not one that would be right for every congregation, but it has worked extremely well at Abundant Life.

Some Christians feel that it is wrong for a congregation to be concerned about numerical growth or that too much emphasis on growth isn't as important as the peace and social justice emphasis of the congregation. We must remember, however, that behind each "number" is a person for whom Christ died. When a Christ-centered church is numerically growing, that church is having an influence for good, helping people one by one to grow and prosper in their spiritual lives.

Generally those churches that grow are those who are meeting the deepest needs of people, that may include spiritual, psychological, emotional, social, and physical needs. The biblical concepts of both salvation and peace or shalom relate to the wholeness of people's lives, not only to spiritual well-being but to overall well-being. Congregations do not grow when they lack a deep concern with the overall well-being of their members and of the community in which the church ministers.

We need to do within our Western culture what overseas missionaries do, which is to ask the question, "What are the needs of the culture around us?" The most basic needs of most people include:

- I need to know that someone cares for me;
- I need to know that my life can have significance in this difficult age; and
- I need something credible in which to put my trust.

One could also summarize those needs by saying they are, respectively, the need to belong, the need to become, and the need to believe. The need to become includes the need to make a difference in the lives of others.

Looking carefully at the needs of people in the community around the church can open the door to creative programs that meet the needs of people and offer them connecting points with the congregation. Those opportunities may include things like:

- Day care for children.
- After school tutoring and meal programs for children.
- Youth recreation programs.
- Groups for people dealing with divorce.
- Marriage enrichment groups.
- Seminars to help parents become better sexuality educators for their teens.

- Support groups for single parents.
- Support groups for people who have lost a child.
- Quilting groups.
- Senior citizen programs.
- Bible study groups.
- Prayer groups.
- Choirs and other musical groups.
- Sexuality education classes for teens.
- Soup kitchens, food pantries, and other programs for the hungry.
- Provision of shelter for the homeless, often in cooperation with other congregations.
- Physical fitness and exercise groups.
- Social groups for young adults.

And so the list can be continued! What are the opportunities to express concern and to meet the needs of people in the area where your church is located?

A Positive Self-Image

"Why would anyone from the community want to come to our church? What do we have to offer others?" mused George, an elder of First Church of the Doldrums, one evening in the congregational outreach committee meeting. "We are stuck back off the main highway and hard to find. Our building needs repair—our restrooms are cold and damp—and we don't have any money to fix anything. We've dropped in attendance in the last 15 years by 150 people. And we argue about what Sunday school curriculum we should be using. Besides that, we've lost a couple of young families in the past two months; the absence of their children has put a real damper on our children's programming."

First Church of the Doldrums, of course is fictitious, but that kind of negative self-perception about the congregation is all too real in many churches. Christian Community often includes the following two items when surveying church members and constituents to evaluate the overall health of a congregation:

- The current morale of the members of this church is very high.

- I am excited about what will happen in the future of this church.

In congregations that are growing, over 90% of those completing a survey will express agreement with both of those items. In congregations in decline, it's not unusual to have agreement drop to as low as 25 to 35%. When people don't feel good about what is happening in the church, it's very difficult for them to reach out with enthusiasm to those outside the church.

Ed Bontrager once became the new pastor of a 75-year-old inner-city church that suffered from very low morale for a number of reasons. The church had gone from 300 members to only 160, and worship attendance was running between 70 and 80. The core members who were still loyal were moving to the suburbs and driving 15 to 20 miles back into the inner city where the church was located. Many had left for other churches.

The church was traditionally Euro-Anglo, but the community was rapidly becoming Latino. The church had started a bus ministry with nominal success. An educational wing built about 15 years earlier now had more than twice the space needed for classes. And overall, the church's self-esteem was low.

Ed and the other church leaders faced a difficult situation. Could they expect that people who left would come back? That rarely happens. Could they reach out to a mosaic community without making adjustments? Obviously not. Rather than continue living with low self-image and low expectations, Ed helped the congregation become proactive, which included:

- Visiting people who lived in the neighborhood around the church to build relationships with them.
- Starting a summer Bible school.
- Revitalizing the bus ministry.
- Using a program called Evangelism Explosion to bring new people into the Kingdom and the church.
- Offering a class in elementary Spanish conducted by the continuing education department of the city.
- Studying how the proper use of spiritual gifts can help growth and assimilation. (See Chapter Five of this book for more information on spiritual gifts.)
- Contracting with a church growth organization for help.

After a couple of years, more people were coming to the church, and those who were coming started to think of it as *their* church rather than as the church of the long-time members only. Carlos and Maria were among the new people who accepted Christ and joined the church. Carlos came to help on workdays. Maria began teaching a children's Sunday school class in Spanish. Soon their grandson and then their daughter became members. New people were becoming assimilated. The church was on the way. One could sense far more positive self-esteem in the congregation. Although the church still had problems, people developed a positive expectation about the future that nurtured continued growth.

A church without a positive self-image will have a tough time easily assimilating new persons. Research has shown that many people who seek a church for the first time, or come to an unfamiliar church after years of absence from any church, are shouldering stress because of some transition in their lives. They may have just moved into the community, given birth to a child, gone through a divorce, or discovered a terminal illness in their family. If a church is struggling with its own difficulties and corporate pain, it will be hard pressed to give much time to a guest or new member who needs healing. New people will more likely be screened rather than assimilated.

This doesn't mean that a church must solve all of its problems before being able to do effective outreach to new people. All churches have some problems, and church leaders continually want to improve the life of the church. It isn't necessary for all problems to be solved for a congregation to develop a positive self-image. It usually is necessary for people in a struggling congregation to begin to feel that proactive steps are being taken to improve the major barriers to effective growth and assimilation of new people.

Sometimes our awareness of the problems in a congregation can cause us to miss the strengths that are present. Steve Clapp did a consultation with a congregation that had low morale because membership and average worship attendance had been declining for almost twenty years. Yet when people started identifying the strengths of their congregation, the list was impressive:

- Most of those who were active in the church had several very close friendships in the congregation and felt cared for by the church in a way they had not experienced in other organizations.
- Everyone was pleased with the quality of the sermons and the pastoral care provided by their minister.
- The church operated a soup kitchen that was well known throughout the community.
- People in the church volunteered at a high level to help with Habitat for Humanity building projects.
- While the church did not have many senior high youth, there was a solid core of middle school youth.

- The church facilities looked a little dated, but everything was in good condition.

The church in fact had plenty to feel good about. Unfortunately, people in the church were not doing a good job inviting others to come to worship or other church activities; and the congregation had not learned how to do a good job opening their social networks to new people. The proactive steps for turning around this congregation included:

- Producing a brochure that highlighted all the strengths of the church that people could give to their friends and that could be used in door-to-door canvassing.
- Holding training in evangelism and hospitality for the entire congregation.
- Scheduling an "Invite a Friend" Sunday to encourage everyone to reach out to people they knew who had no church home.
- Holding more social events for the middle school youth and encouraging them to invite their friends.
- Using a service to obtain the names of new people who moved into the neighborhood around the church and reaching out to those persons.

Reaching Out to All People

Many factors can be responsible for people beginning to attend a church. In some instances, people have relocated from another community, have a history of congregational involvement, and want to become part of another church. Sometimes people have experienced a crisis or a difficult transition in their lives and become interested in church in a way they have not been in the past. Often the motivation to try out a congregation comes because a friend, family member, or coworker in that congregation has encouraged a person or family to start coming.

Sometimes people have had a painful experience in another congregation and are seeking a new church home.

Whatever the reasons that cause an individual or family to start coming, the continuation of that involvement can't be taken for granted. There are three major stages in the first year of a person's involvement in a new congregation, and whether or not that person continues to be involved depends on the experiences at each stage.

- The first couple of months are the entry process. Dropouts in this period are often the result of mixed motivations on their initially coming, on a lack of follow-up by the pastor or the church when these people visit, or on a perception that the church just is not warm or is not theologically compatible.

- The second period comes in the third to eighth months when new people begin asking the relationship-need questions. "Can I develop friends in this church? Who have I really learned to know? Where do I fit in socially? Am I needed?" If the social networks of the church are open, they will have positive answers to these questions, and their involvement will deepen.

- The third period comes somewhere around the ninth to twelfth months. "Do I feel cared for with greater compassion by the church than in other important relationships in my life? Does the church meet my needs? Is my contribution valued?" What began as a theological quest—getting help from God for this critical time in one's life—transitions into relational needs.

The majority of people who become inactive begin to do so within the first year of their involvement. Christian Community's research shows that 62% of those who start attending a church are less active twelve months later than at the start. If new people can make it through the first twelve months with steady involvement, the chance of them remaining active in- creases significantly.

The people we seek to integrate into our churches are sometimes very similar to those who are already members; but if our outreach is truly effective, we will be integrating into the church some people who are different. Throughout the Gospels we see Jesus reaching out to politicians, tax collectors, known sinners, lepers, and women—all people who were marginalized in society, especially by the religious leaders of the day, the Scribes and Pharisees. In Luke 7:36–8:3 Jesus reached out to a woman held in contempt by most of society—a prostitute. She had probably listened to Jesus from the edge of the crowd, and realized that he was the one who could lift from her the burden of guilt and disgrace. Jesus felt no further need to preach at her or to condemn her, but rather reached out to her, allowing her to wash his feet with her tears, and anoint them with a phial of concentrated perfume.

When Jesus commissioned us to reach all people, including the troubled, the helpless, and those living without hope, he was not giving us an easy task. Certainly most of our churches find it easiest to assimilate people who come as transfers and have been previously active in other congregations. Those persons come with at least some knowledge of the Bible, an understanding of the church, and generally a high level of commitment. Churches that truly reach out to those with no past church connection will find some of their work difficult but also very rewarding.

A willingness to accept all people is central to effective outreach. One church Ed pastored had as its tagline: "The Church of All People." In that congregation, "all people" included those of both Latino and Anglo descent, persons who were mentally challenged, and persons from assisted living homes near the church.

At another church Ed pastored, the outreach committee consisted of the following: a person who had left a sexually promiscuous lifestyle; a twice-divorced woman who had been living with a man for a few years and had been on drugs; a divorced woman who had her life threatened by her adopted daughter; and another person who had used drugs. These persons had all been accepted by the congregation and had made drastic lifestyle changes. Their love for God and a changed life went hand-in-hand. Another of the persons on the committee was a retired bishop, who was also positively accepted by the church!

A church that does well at including others has members who are willing to take time to get outside their own comfort zones and are not afraid of relating to people who are different from them. The church of all people needs loving Christians who see people unlike themselves through the eyes of Jesus. Our job is to love people and provide for their basic needs as much as possible.

It's also important to remember that we cannot assimilate people into the church without being assimilated into their lives too. They may find some things about those of us who are already active in the congregation just as difficult to accept as we may find some of their characteristics. It's easy for people in the church to come across as judgmental, too focused on the past, and unwilling to truly open our social circles to new people. We need to be aware of some of the barriers to assimilation, discussed in the next section.

Obstacles to Assimilation

Existing friendships and family ties. Established churches are sometimes blessed with people who have been in the same church all their lives. Since it is generally true that individuals are socially and emotionally able to maintain only a small number of close friendships, these long-term church members had their pick long ago. Why would they want anyone new in their circle? Their psychological and social needs seem to them already fulfilled.

To become acquainted with someone new, to invite her over for tea, or meet him for coffee, or to attend a sports event together are all nice ideas. But why would anyone choose to spend time with someone they don't really know well? Why would they want to make that person a substitute for a long-time friend? But this kind of thinking misses the essence of hospitality and also misses the reality that new friendships are potential blessings to our lives.

Our best friends were once strangers to us. By avoiding or locking out the stranger, we may in fact be locking out the blessings of God:

> Do not neglect to show hospitality to strangers, for by doing that some have entertained angels without knowing it.
>
> **Hebrews 13:2**

Hospitality to the stranger is assumed throughout the Old and New Testament Scriptures. Again and again, as in the Parable of the Good Samaritan, the questioning is not on the worthiness of the stranger but on the faithfulness of the one encountering the stranger. The Samaritan did not ask of the man who was injured: "Did you bring this on yourself? Were you trying to do a drug deal? Why weren't you traveling with someone else for safety?" The Samaritan simply responded to the human need that was encountered. The priest and the Levite who passed by are the ones whose behavior is called into question by our Lord's telling of the parable. Look once more at the core definitions of this book:

> **Hospitality** is the **attitude** and **practice** of providing the **atmosphere** and **opportunities**, however risky, in which strangers are free to become friends, thereby feeling accepted, included, and loved. The relationship thus opens up the possibility for eventual communion among the host, the stranger, and God.

> **Hospitality** involves recognizing the presence of Christ in family, friends, coworkers, neighbors, and complete strangers. It means responding to others as we would respond to the presence of Christ in our midst.

Whether we start with the assumption that the unknown person will be an enemy or a friend makes a difference! When anyone comes to our church or shows an interest in religious concerns, our starting assumption certainly should be that such a person shares with us a pull toward the heart of God. Such a person is a potential friend, perhaps sent to us by God for the enrichment of our lives.

Think how your view of the new person in your neighborhood, your office, or the church would be transformed if your starting assumption was:

> *This is a person sent by God who may be a great blessing to my life, or this is a person sent by God in order for me to be a blessing to his or her life.*

Obviously such blessings have a tendency to flow in both directions!

Denominationalism and history. Some congregations seem more interested in the past than in the future. The illustrations in the pastor's messages often refer to cherished traditions. The Sunday school rooms are named for historical characters of that denomination. There's nothing wrong with that, but these names of past saints need to be explained to new attendees. Bulletin announcements have code words, abbreviations and acronyms that are known only by those who have been in the denomination or church for years.

Leaders in a church of German descent thought they could help maintain their tradition by labeling their restroom doors, "Versleit" and "Monsleit." Though German or Pennsylvania Dutch was not the language of the younger generation, the boys and girls who grew up in the church knew which one to choose. But what about the guests? One day someone got a revelation! Will our guests know which is which? How embarrassing if they don't! They moved into the era of English usage and changed the signs.

When Christians move from one city to another, over 50% of these persons have no problem switching denominations. They go where the members of their family discover programs and services that will minister to them. Or they are seeking out a certain type of worship style. Or they prefer driving only one or two miles to an interdenominational church rather than driving 30 miles to attend a church of their own denomination.

This brings up the subject of how much can be sacrificed in order to reach people. Do we give up our denominational moorings and certain aspects of our theology? Do we change our worship traditions? Do we come up with a church name that leaves out our denominational name in order to appeal to more people? There are no easy answers to these questions. But excessive denominationalism can hinder assimilation. Each congregation needs to look at these questions in the light of their purpose and overall vision. Sometimes it means consulting with their judicatory or denominational office. However, the church that wishes to be culturally relevant will seriously consider these questions.

One church that followed a three-year process called Living in Faithful Evangelism (LIFE), which helped transition congregations into more effective outreach, shared this testimony. "Incorporating new members into the family of God is not an easy process, we are finding. It requires us to change, to let go of some cherished patterns and ways of doing things in order to give new people ownership in God's family. But the exciting thing is, it's not just the new people who receive new Life! Our whole congregation is being given new Life!"

We've always done it this way! Those words, closely related to the barriers of excessive denominationalism or emphasis on history, can keep newer members from feeling that they have significant input into the life of the church. We've all heard people say, in response to a suggestion for change, "But we've always done it this way!"

In truth, there are often good reasons why things are done in a particular way in a congregation. The flow of the worship service, the handling of a major fund-raising event, and the structure of an annual retreat have often evolved over time and do a good job meeting the needs of people.

Newer members, however, have not had the opportunity to be part of that process in the past and may look at things in a new way. While their suggestions won't always represent improvement, those who have been members for longer periods of time need to listen with openness to new ideas. When newer members want a change that doesn't create a problem, there are benefits to going along with the change. And sometimes their new perspective will result in significant improvements if those of us who have been around for more years can be genuinely open.

In the area of worship, we need to be especially open to the suggestions of new people. Newer members often have greater awareness of how people outside the church would respond to our services of worship. The changes that would make newer members more comfortable with worship may also be changes that would make services more attractive to people outside the congregation. The book *Worship and Hospitality* by Steve Clapp and Fred Bernhard discusses change in worship more thoroughly than is possible in this publication.

A reputation of tension and strife. The antennae of new people can readily pick up the sound waves of dissension among members. First-time guests will not stay around long if they see that the church is bogged down by internal conflicts, gossiping, or a lack of moral integrity among leadership. These fiascos and failures can happen from time to time in any congregation. We know that the Corinthian church in the Apostle Paul's time was notorious for all kinds of sins and offenses. The fact that these failures are common, however, does not make them any more healthy or any less a barrier to new people.

Ed Bontrager shares this account of the problems with a turnaround program in one congregation. This had been a church where "the young people were in their fifties" and 20% of the members were 80 and above. Joe, who was twenty-something, had fallen away from the Lord and the church, but he started coming back. It was not long until he and his fiancée, Marie, came to the pastor to be married. It was a nice wedding—many people from the church came and gave them their support. Joe and Marie became very involved in the church. And soon Joe was voted in as assistant board chair—it seemed like a good assimilation process . . . until one dreadful evening.

At a board meeting with twenty people in attendance, an argument took place between George (who was the board chair) and another couple—these people had experienced other disagreements over the years. In a display of anger, George said to his wife Kathryn, who was also present, "Let's get out of here!" They left the meeting. Joe, who was very new to the position of assistant chair, had to take over the meeting in the face of the tremendous tension left by George and Kathryn leaving. He did well that evening, as he worked to pick up the pieces; but Joe and Marie began to discover that there were many tense relationships in the church. They left the congregation.

There is no perfect church, or else very few of us would fit in! Some tensions and disagreements are inevitable in any gathering of people, including the church. When disagreements and tensions become commonplace, however, the ability to assimilate new people is seriously compromised. A church cannot grow when stress and negativism push out peace and a positive spirit.

Should Churches Draw a Line?

The church in the twenty-first century sometimes finds itself in a dilemma. We desire a church of all people, and want to follow the example of Christ whose ministry went outside the ecclesiastical lines rigidly set by a Pharisaic collection of rules and regulations. As we scan the religious landscape we find some churches that are willing to do just that as they reach out to prostitutes, those with substance abuse and other addictions, and felons. Some churches have set up prison ministries and halfway houses, with church members ministering to ex-convicts, and helping them transition as they work to become responsible people in the community once again.

Congregational or denominational beliefs and traditions raise questions for some about that kind of broad acceptance. Is there a difference between initial acceptance and ongoing membership? If a congregation is expected to follow the Bible interpreted through a set of doctrinal statements or a confession of faith, do we sidestep these doctrines so we can welcome everyone? Do we fully integrate as members those whose lifestyle and practice differ from what many in the church find acceptable? There should be no question about the worth of all people and about the kind of broad hospitality our churches should show to all who come. But is there a time to draw a line? Are there ethical and moral requirements for persons who wish to identify as a full members of a congregation?

We need to recognize that all of us have sinned and are dependent on the grace of God for our salvation. People who have ended up in prison for felony convictions or who have spent time in a halfway house with drug problems have sins that are more obvious. Those of us who sit comfortably in the pew on Sunday morning, however, also have areas of struggle. Sometimes people with substance abuse problems and people who are sexually unfaithful do such a good job covering up what is happening in their lives that those around them are not aware of what they are doing. Then there are the problems of jealousy, greed, anger, gossip, and passive-aggressive behavior, which afflict many of us in congregational life.

Those of us who look honestly at our own lives will generally find it more difficult to be judgmental toward others. The church needs primarily to be concerned when a new potential member or even a long-time member has shown evidence of behaviors that could pose risks for others in the congregation.

People who do not have a history of church involvement seek out the church because someone in the congregation has reached out to them or because they are seeking a deeper connection with God and with other people. Their interest in coming to the church often grows out of a deep desire to improve their lives including their relationships with other people and with God.

Sometimes people who are deeply ashamed of how they have lived come to church horribly afraid of how people there will respond to them. They are hungry for acceptance, and they are open to change within an accepting community.

A friend of Ed's named Barry had used drugs for years, served time in prison, and generally made a mess of his life. He started changing his life and began to run a successful business (though he still had some problems with back taxes!). His wife told him about a phone call asking if they would like to receive information about a new church that was being started in the neighborhood. Feeling they had nothing to lose, they accepted the literature, though they made no immediate response to it.

For reasons he did not fully understand, Barry became convinced that he should be giving significant money, perhaps a full tithe (10%) to a charity. He had no church of his own, but remembered his wife receiving the call about a new church. Barry got the address from the literature, wrote out a check, but took a felt-tipped black marker and covered over his own name and address. He scrawled his signature on the check. He did not want any religious fanatic from any church group bothering him.

When the check arrived, John, the pastor, was curious. Who as an outsider would write a check for such a substantial amount to a church? Why would the person cover over his name? He held the check up to the light, and with little problem saw the name, address, and telephone number. He decided to risk a phone call, wanting to make a connection with this unknown benefactor.

John thanked Barry and then asked if they could get together for coffee soon. Hesitantly Barry agreed. However, Barry asked on the phone, "I smoke, would you allow me into your church?" John responded, "Yes." "I drink, would that keep me out?" "No," said Pastor John. Barry continued with more questions.

Barry later shared, "In all these positions, John simply indicated that he was at a different place than I was, and that it was possible some of my positions might change in time. In theological terms, John did not allow any of these issues to be a litmus test for orthodoxy. Instead, he stressed the primacy of Jesus as we submit to Him."

Barry and John met not only once, but many, many times, and now Barry is an active member of that congregation, having discovered that Jesus can change lives. With his back taxes paid, and drugs and other vices behind, Barry lives out a life of faith, and is a witness to the power of God. However, it took a pastor and people to accept him where he was and walk with him to a better and more fulfilling life.

Some worship services include a sharing time. There have been instances where those who seem to have hostile traits or whose character is questionable will get up, and make statements that can cause a dark pall to settle over what was a vital, meaningful service. Ed and Steve have both been in services where people who were not mentally healthy interrupted services with comments and shouts that were not appreciated by others. In such cases church leaders need to confront with kindness persons who don't realize they are making it difficult for others to connect with the worship service. Sometimes people need to be pulled aside and kindly encouraged to share their feelings and needs in more appropriate settings than worship.

There are tragic situations in which sexual predators have taken advantage of people in the church. In our society there are men who make inappropriate overtures to women, and the reverse can also be true. There are people of both genders who have done inappropriate things to children and young people. The scandals in the Roman Catholic Church have made us aware that the church has not always fulfilled its obligation to keep people safe. Those risks are not confined to the Roman Catholic

Church—they are very real for all congregations. We do need to be concerned about keeping everyone safe in the faith community.

What should the stance of the church be regarding sexual offenders? Turning away a person who discloses that he is a sex offender may drive him to another congregation and discourage him from disclosing the next time. The offender who isn't known, but who has children's trust, poses a greater threat to children than a known sex offender. Ideally, parents and children should already be educated about the prevention of child abuse, but steps can be taken to preclude a person's contact with children while still inviting their participation in some church activities. The support of a church community can reduce the isolation and increase the accountability of a potential congregant, and as such can decrease the chance of another offense.

One way to allow the participation of offenders would be to agree that they are welcome in gatherings only attended by adults, but will be monitored during worship times and fellowship activities that would include people of all ages. Any contact with children would be prohibited. If these persons intend to continue in the church, even with these conditions, they need to be asked to seek out a therapist who is a member of ATSA, the Association for the Treatment of Sexual Abusers, if they are not already doing so. A further caring act by the church would be to help pay for such services, if there is a need for this help.

Much more information on the safe involvement of sex offenders in faith communities can be found in *A Time to Heal*, by Rev. Debra W. Haffner.

When visiting in Turkey in the biblical city of Iconium (now named Konya), Ed saw a plaque with a quote by a thirteenth-century Muslim philosopher, the founder of the Whirling Dervish sect, which says, "Come, come again, whoever, whatever you may be, come; heathen fire worshiper, sinful of idolatry, come, come even if you broke your penitence a hundred times, ours is not the portal of misery and despair, come." As Christians engaged in mission to others, we also say, "Come—come whoever you may be, whatever your background, come. Come to taste and see that the Lord is good. We who are of the Lord and His church, we welcome you into His fold. Come and follow Him and be His disciple."

Characteristics of Assimilated Persons

The following list of characteristics can help you in determining how assimilated people are into the life of the church.

Characteristics of Assimilated Persons
1.   They are enthusiastic about their faith commitment and the congregation, and they feel they are in a loving place.
2.   They feel their relationship to God is strengthened and nurtured in the church.
3.   They have a personal relationship with the pastor(s) (depending on the size of the congregation). They know at least six or seven persons in the congregation whom they can identify as their friends.
4.   They attend worship at least three times per month.

5. They are regularly giving financially to the church.

6. They are involved in a small group.

7. They have a meaningful role/task appropriate to their spiritual gifts.

8. They are sharing their faith with unchurched friends and family.

9. They have faith in the future of their church and are loyal to its ministry.

Who are the Forgotten?

If your church is serious about broadening its outreach and extending its welcome, it can be helpful to think about persons who are in the community who are not currently involved in your congregation.

The following exercise, from *Reaching the Forgotten*, by Steve Clapp, Julie Seibert Berman, Pat Helman and Cindy Hollenberg Snider, is designed to help you think about various categories of persons relative to their activity or potential activity in your congregation. Those which you mark **NC** are the ones who may have been forgotten or overlooked in past outreach efforts of the congregation. (You have our permission to reproduce this exercise for use in your church.)

IC   Persons who are already active *in your church*.

NC   Persons who are present in the neighborhood or ministry area of your congregation but who are *not in your church* or at least not in numbers proportionate to their population in the community.

NF   Persons *not found* in your church or in your church's neighborhood or ministry area

____   Retired persons
____   Divorced persons
____   Young married couples
____   Teenagers
____   The Deaf
____   Persons with impaired mobility (confined to wheelchairs, severe arthritis, etc.)
____   Persons with learning disabilities
____   Single male adults
____   Single female adults
____   Persons who are wealthy
____   Persons who are poor
____   Persons with advanced degrees
____   Persons with little formal education
____   Children in foster care or institutions
____   Parents of infants and small children
____   Parents of teenagers
____   College students
____   Members of the military
____   Voluntary service participants
____   White people
____   African Americans
____   Asian Americans
____   Latino people

_____ Native Americans
_____ Gay, lesbian and bisexual people
_____ Transgender people
_____ Childless couples
_____ Alcoholics
_____ Persons who have to work on Sundays
_____ Persons who find it hard to mix with others and make new friends
_____ Persons who have obvious physical disfigurement
_____ Persons of different political views than most of the congregation
_____ Persons who disapprove of drinking and/or smoking
_____ Persons who drink and/or smoke
_____ Persons suffering from terminal illness or other serious health problems
_____ Persons caring for someone who suffers from terminal illness or other serious health problems
_____ Persons who are struggling to grow spiritually
_____ Persons who want to help the hungry and the homeless
_____ The hungry and homeless
_____ Persons who dislike traditional worship services
_____ Persons who dislike contemporary worship services
_____ Persons who have an extremely high need for feedback on the volunteer work they do
_____ Persons who are afraid of crowds
_____ Persons with serious emotional problems
_____ Persons with a loved one having serious emotional problems
_____ Persons recovering from alcoholism or other drug addiction
_____ Persons with a loved one who is recovering from alcoholism or other drug addiction
_____ Persons who have been damaged by the occult
_____ Persons who have been damaged by the church
_____ Persons who are opposed to any kind of church involvement in political affairs

_____ Persons who believe the church should be actively involved in political affairs

_____ Persons who want to participate in social activities that will help them make new friends

_____ Young parents who need child care in order to participate in worship services or Sunday school

_____ Single parents

_____ Families who want church activities that keep them together as a family (rather than dividing them by age and sex)

_____ Persons who are concerned about the welfare of animals

_____ Persons who have been to prison

_____ Persons who have family members in prison

_____ Persons who have been victims of crime

Remember that true hospitality

is not just another program

of the church.

True hospitality must flow

through all that your church does

and must be part of the lives

of the members.

Chapter Four
The Price of Assimilation

Ephesians 2:19–22

Concept: **Services and products in our society come with a price. Successfully welcoming and involving new people in the church does not come without some expenditure of what people have valued in the past. The price of assimilation is change.**

It's not unusual for people to visit a large number of congregations before they find one that feels comfortable, where they feel truly accepted. Kristen Leverton Helbert, a Christian Community employee, and her husband Chad had that experience when they moved to Toledo, Ohio, following their marriage. Kristen was already working for Christian Community and had been a part of some of the organization's research projects on factors that cause people to want to return to churches. She knew that growing churches very often have a person go to the home of first-time visitors within forty-eight hours of their attendance and take them a plate of cookies, a loaf of bread, or some other kind of welcoming gift.

As she and Chad attended church after church, they found the welcome at the churches highly variable and the follow-up almost nonexistent. Kristen once remarked to Steve Clapp, "We've been to seven churches, and I'm still waiting for the cookies to appear at the door." Their warmest welcome came from a relatively large congregation in a denominational tradition different from the ones in which Kristen and Chad had grown up. They felt quickly accepted and wanted in the life of the church.

Megan and her husband had a similar experience. Here's how she explained it to Ed Bontrager: "We arrived in the area in late January and spent 18 months looking for a church. We visited a church every Sunday and sometimes returned to those that were promising. However, none seemed to be quite right. I had repeatedly searched the phone book looking for new prospects. We did not consider Faith Community immediately because... we were familiar with the denominational tradition, and knew that we had a different understanding regarding the military. Finally, we decided to give Faith Community a try."

She continued, "We thought we would at least visit, simply because we had ruled out other churches as possibilities. I some-times jokingly say we came to Faith Community out of desper-ation, but, in truth, that really was the case. However, I remem-ber thinking that first Sunday, as I was sitting on the back row meeting people, 'This feels right. This feels like where we belong.'"

Though this couple had known no one in Faith Community before they visited, they felt a warm welcome and an immediate acceptance. Megan says, "The congregation was friendly. They spoke and introduced themselves. We had actually visited one church in the area where no one spoke to us—not a single person. We even had to get our own bulletins. And it was an early service with a small crowd, so it wasn't as though visitors wouldn't be noticed. Needless to say, we didn't go back."

There is a myth that small churches are just naturally friendlier and that large churches are colder. While small congregations certainly have a potential advantage in the initial welcome because there is no difficulty determining who are visitors and who are already members, the truth is that many small congregations are too inwardly turned and that some very large congregations know how to convey warmth and accept-ance. Christian Community's research does not find success at welcoming new people correlated with size of the congregation! It does relate to the percentage of people in the congregation who are willing to take the initiative in reaching out to new people and to whether or not the congregation has a clear plan for visitor follow-up.

Check the Welcoming System

Ed Bontrager once visited more than twenty churches in a short period of time, taking along a checklist and observing as unobtrusively as possible what the congregations did to help people feel welcome or unwelcome. He kept track of traditional measures like greeters by the doors, the friendliness of ushers, the warmth of other members, and a follow-up within a day or so of attending. But he also looked for parking lot attendants, clear directions to restrooms, the usability of bulletins (free of any unfamiliar acronyms or unclear instructions), and whether or not he was assisted in finding a place to sit. At one church he inadvertently sat in the area normally reserved for teenagers!

At another church, Ed couldn't find the main entrance. He looked all around the church without success. Then he returned to the front, pushed aside an empty five-gallon paint bucket, and found a flight of stairs. What a surprise he had when he went up the stairs and burst through the door into the front of the sanctuary! The meeting place was only temporary in this new church plant—this second-story hall was actually used for dance instruction during the week. Since it was only temporary, the leadership may have not thought through what it takes to make a good first impression for people seeking a new church. They at least needed to think about a sign clearly indicating that the sanctuary was at the top of the flight of stairs, and the paint bucket belonged somewhere else!

In another congregation, people leaving Sunday school walked past Ed on their way to the sanctuary without giving him any greeting. But in other churches he found the opposite—friendliness, acceptance, clear signs and directions, helpful greeters and ushers, and information about the church and its programs.

Check the welcoming system of your congregation. When you visit a church for the first time, what are you looking for? Put into practice those things that you personally would want to find if you were seeking a new church home.

Pastor Leslie Francisco of Calvary Community Church in Hampton, Virginia, tells about a man who became a vital part of the church saying to him, "I need to tell you that I didn't begin coming to Calvary because of you. I'll tell you how it came about. When I first visited the church, a man with an umbrella came outside to help me get into the church. Then a woman with a big welcoming smile, who was a greeter, gave me a bulletin and showed me where the sanctuary was. Then I met two ushers who welcomed me warmly and seated me. I knew before I heard one word from you that this is where I wanted to come." Calvary Church understands the rule that you never have a second chance to make a good first impression.

The welcome, of course, must go beyond the work of greeters and ushers to include all the people who interact with guests. Friendliness is one thing; forming friendships is another. We all know that friendliness is the first step—the forming of friendships is the glue.

Why are friendships important? Because people want to feel accepted and to share with others as they seek to grow in their faith and to make sense of their lives. If a person attends church for a few Sundays and people merely say "Hello" in passing, going on to talk with their own longtime friends, the guest correctly perceives that he or she is not really wanted. One price tag for assimilation is the expansion of our friendship circles to include new people.

Do Guests Know You Are Expecting Company?

How prepared is your church for guests? This checklist can help you do an initial evaluation:

1. Do you have attractive, well-placed signs that welcome guests, as well as show the times of services? ___Yes ___No
2. Do you have parking lot attendants? ___Yes ___No
3. Is your entrance to the main gathering area or lobby clearly marked? ___Yes ___No
4. Do you have greeters by the outside doors? ___Yes ___No
5. Do you provide first-time visitors with a brochure that gives significant information about your church? ___Yes ___No
6. Do you give out a small appreciation gift? ___Yes ___No
7. Do you have signs that help visitors locate restrooms, the nursery, classrooms, and the sanctuary? ___Yes ___No
8. Have you developed an appropriate procedure for finding out names and other vital information from guests?* ___Yes ___No
9. Do you have trained ushers, especially sensitive to the needs of guests? ___Yes ___No
10. Are your people generally outgoing and friendly to guests? ___Yes ___No
11. Do people readily introduce guests to others? ___Yes ___No
12. Are people assisted in finding a place to sit? ___Yes ___No
13. Does the pastor or worship leader remember to extend a special welcome to guests who are in the audience (without making them stand and be publicly introduced)?** ___Yes ___No

14. Do you include, as part of the worship service, a few moments when attendees can informally greet others around them? ___Yes ___No

15. Is your bulletin attractive, and can guests readily understand it? ___Yes ___No

16. Is your worship service positive, uplifting, dynamic, and moving? ___Yes ___No

17. Are words to the Lord's Prayer, the Doxology, and any other parts of the liturgy in print for the benefit of guests who may not be familiar with them? ___Yes ___No

18. Do you have greeters or others who can help guests find the best Sunday school class or small group opportunity for them? ___Yes ___No

19. Are guests shown caring hospitality in your Sunday school classes or small groups? ___Yes ___No

20. Do members frequently ask guests to join them for Sunday brunch or for another meal? ___Yes ___No

21. Does the pastor greet all participants as they leave after church? ___Yes ___No

22. Is a follow-up letter sent by the pastor or lay person to all first-time guests? ___Yes ___No

23. Are guests called upon in their homes by congregational members within a day or two following their attendance at worship or another congregational activity? ___Yes ___No

* Follow-up with guests is, of course, impossible without a street address, e-mail address, or phone number. This information can be obtained through a guest registration process with pads or forms provided in the pews and members as well as guests completing the information. Passing the pad or form back down the pew lets people know the names of those seated near them. Some churches handle this by a registration book when people arrive or by gathering the information at a Welcoming Table. Another option is including a card in the bulletin for people to complete and place in the offering plate.

** Christian Community's research shows that two out of three guests do not like to be put on the spot with a formal introduction to the whole congregation. They want to be warmly greeted by those seated near them, but they don't feel comfortable being introduced to the whole church.

Benefits of the Drop-By Visit

Guests want to feel a warm welcome, and they want to know that the social networks of the congregation are open to new people. They do not, however, want to feel smothered. Here's what one person shared with Ed Bontrager: "I remember what happened to us in Georgia. We had just moved in on Friday, visited a church on Sunday, and it was now Monday night. The house was still in disarray and we got a call from someone from the church we had gone to on Sunday wanting to come by that evening for a visit. My husband took the call and tried to tell the person that we just weren't ready to have visitors. This person, however, was insistent and told us he would see us shortly.

"The person came; we were polite; and we ended up not going to that church. We got the impression that we were just names on a list that it was his responsibility to check off. He didn't care about our needs or what would work best for us. He only seemed to care that he had visited all these people. Had he been willing to come a week or so later, we would have been happy to talk with him as we were interested in his church initially."

Christian Community's research shows that the best follow-up calls to the homes of people following their initial visit to a congregation are ones that are made without an appointment. If no one is at home, the cookies, bread, or other welcoming gift are left at the door with a short note or a card. If someone is home, the person or persons making the visit make no request to come inside. They simply say they are from the church, haven't come to stay for a visit, but wanted to thank them for coming and to give them a small gift. A brochure of more information about the church should generally be shared along with the gift. If people choose to invite them inside to visit, that is fine; but the expectation should be for the conversation to take place at the door.

When phone calls are made in advance of the visit, it can feel to people as though the church is pressuring them to make a decision about membership, which is certainly not what one wants them to experience. The "drop by" visit avoids creating discomfort. There are very few people who aren't pleased to receive a loaf of bread or a plate of cookies! An appointment, of course, should be made before any future visit that is intended to be more substantial in nature.

Remembering Names and Building Relationships

While we won't know every single person in a very large congregation, we most certainly want to know as many as possible. And names are important. Knowing the name of a person is a first step in understanding and valuing that person.

Name tags are a valuable part of the welcoming system in all but the very smallest congregations. In congregations of more than 80–120 members, even the regulars don't know everyone. If the name tags for guests have a different shape or appearance than the members' name tags, the guests can be easily identified and special welcomes given.

Even in a small congregation, name tags can be a help to guests. If a church has an average worship attendance of only 25–40 people, those who are members will have no difficulty at all recognizing guests; and the flow of guests generally will not be so high that it's difficult to remember names. The guest, however, is faced with trying to remember the names of 25–40 people, which is not an easy task!

One pastor, who has several guests in the congregation every Sunday, keeps what he calls a "cheat sheet" in his Bible, where he writes down the names of new attendees immediately after each worship service, so he can review the names during the week and again just before the following week's worship services. More than once he has heard, "I came back and the pastor remembered my name!"

Here are some other tips to help remember the names of guests in worship and work toward building relationships with them, depending on your role in the congregation:

- Many churches, as noted earlier in this chapter, have a pad or card in each pew with a place for people to enter their names and addresses. The pad or card is passed from person-to-person along the row and then returned back to the starting point for collection by an usher. When the pad or card is passed back down the row, people have an opportunity to view the names of others in their row. This gives a "first exposure" to the names of people one does not know. At the end of the worship service, taking the initiative to greet that person and to use his or her name can help with remembering it.

- Greeters and ushers can more effectively remember the names of guests when they intentionally use the names in conversation with that person. For example:

  Greeter: "Good morning. I'm Joe Wallace, and it's my pleasure to welcome you to our worship service this morning."
  Guest: "I'm Helen Fleming, and I'm glad to be here."

Greeter: "Helen, I'm glad that you've come. The entrance to the sanctuary is just to your right. Is there anything else that I can do to help you?"
Guest: "No, thanks."
Greeter: "I hope you enjoy the service, Helen. We have a wonderful choir and a great minister."

The repetition of the name helps most people remember it longer, and those who are guests feel good about the use of the name.

* Another way to both reinforce the name and start to build a relationship with the other person is to make a point of calling the guest on the phone sometime in the first couple of days after the worship service.

* Everyone can benefit from the pastor's "cheat sheet" concept by writing down the name or names of guests (perhaps in the margin of the bulletin) and then reviewing those names during the week and immediately prior to the next week's worship service.

* If you don't remember a person's name, don't feel embarrassed. When you see that person the next time, introduce yourself again, acknowledge that you don't remember the person's name, and then use it immediately after being told again. Write it down later, and you'll be far more likely to remember it the next time.

* Greenmonte Church in Stuarts Draft, Virginia, has a group called GEM, which stands for Greemonte Encouragement Ministry. The GEM group of three to six people, including the pastor, writes personal notes to guests following their visit. A group member drops by the guest's home briefly with a small gift. Others write notes the second week. The pastor of the church says that

90% of visitors come back. Guests are impressed by the handwritten notes and by the short visits. This process also guarantees that a group of people will remember the names of guests.

- Introduce new participants in the church newsletter or through a bulletin insert. This shouldn't be done after the first visit but can be done whenever the guest appears to be making attendance a habit. The same can be done electronically if your church uses an e-mail newsletter. Ask the person for permission before listing his or her name. Conduct an interview if the new participant is willing, and share information in the newsletter or bulletin insert.

- If your church has a pictorial directory, print additions to it when several guests have begun participating. The quality of computer software and printers makes this far easier and less expensive than in the past. You may wish to designate a church photographer to take photographs of guests who are ready to be listed.

- Some congregations post pictures of guests on a bulletin board, but you want to be sure not to do this without permission. It's generally better to wait until people join to post their pictures in a public place. Having a picture posted is less comfortable to most people than an addition being made to a pictorial directory.

- Hold a periodic "Guess Who's Coming For Dinner." This is an event for which volunteers are recruited who are willing to entertain six to eight people from the church with a dinner in their homes. People in the church are given opportunity to indicate their willingness to take part in a dinner on a particular night. The "guess who's coming" part is that the hosts know how many guests will come but not their identities. Those who are coming know the home to which they are to go but do not know who else is coming besides the person or persons hosting the dinner. The organizers of the event work hard to mix newer members with long-time members of the church.

• Members of the church should develop the habit of inviting guests to join them for lunch, brunch, or dinner. (This concept is so important that you'll find it repeated at various points in this book.)

• Give guests a church mailbox after three or four visits, if your church provides this service.

• If you have a sharing time in your worship service, make sure that people give their full name before they speak. This is especially important in smaller congregations in which members too often assume that everyone knows everyone. Guests do not!

Friendship Partners or Faith Friends

Some friendships may form spontaneously, especially with guests who already have family, friendship, vocational, or neighborhood connections with others in the church. But what happens when new people move into your area from another state because of a job transfer? What about college students who are new to the area? What about people who are long-time residents of the community but happen to not know anyone in the congregation? When there are no previous or natural links with people in the congregation, extra care needs to be taken to help guests develop meaningful connections and friendships.

A ministry of "friendship partners" or "faith friends" can help integrate new people. The friendship partner or faith friend concept has an individual, couple, or family adopting or mentoring a new individual, couple, or family for the first year or so of their involvement in the congregation. They continue this special relationship until a coordinator feels the new people are well assimilated into congregational life.

The "coordinator of faith friends" or "coordinator of assimilation" selects and appoints the faith friends and links them with guests or new members at an appropriate time, usually when the new person has begun what looks like a potentially regular pattern of attendance, perhaps for three or four weeks. A faith friend or friendship partner should never be forced on a prospective member, but almost all will welcome this link to the church.

Occasionally long-time church members in smaller congregations react unenthusiastically to this type of programming. Their perception of their church is that it is a friendly group of people, so these relationships will just happen spontaneously. Unfortunately, even in small congregations, that isn't always the case. In medium-sized and large congregations, a faith friend or friendship partner program can play an extremely important role.

There are several things faith friends can do to help with the assimilation of guests, prospective members, and new members:

1. Pray for faith friends daily by name. Include everyone in the family.

2. Offer social connections with new people outside the church setting. Faith friends can invite guests into their home for a backyard barbeque, supper, or dessert. Invite just the individual, couple, or family the first time. Then consider inviting them to come again and adding to the group a few others from the church who are likely to be enjoyed by the guests.

3. Make a point of introducing the new person to others in the congregation so that the web of connections is expanded for that person. Sit with or near the new person for a couple of weeks to make it easier to introduce that person to others. If the guest is a single person rather than part of a couple or family, sitting with someone in church is often more comfortable than sitting alone.

4. If they miss two services in a row, give them a phone call or send an e-mail—not as a truancy officer!—but to express regret that you did not see them. Usually you will learn about an illness, travel, or guests in their home. They will appreciate knowing that they were missed; and if something unpleasant has happened in the church, the faith friend can respond and help.

5. Seek to involve the guest, your friend, in appropriate church activities such as the women's or men's fellowship, youth group, choir, church picnic, a Sunday school class, a Bible study group, or a book club. Consider the possibility of driving them to the function or of meeting them there. Knowing another person makes it easier to merge into a new group.

6. Discover and find ways to utilize the gifts and talents of the guest or new member in the ministry of the church. Connect the new person with service opportunities in the congregation. This might mean involvement with the music program, helping with a Christian education class, working with the youth group, or helping with a Habitat for Humanity project. This process is made easier if your church has a spiritual gifts program, as described in the next chapter.

7. If you find the guest or new member asking for help with the devotional life or with questions about personal faith, respond as you feel comfortable. You don't have to have all the answers. In some instances, you may want to refer the person to a pastor, another staff member, or an experienced Sunday school

teacher. In other instances, you may want to share devotional resources that your church offers like copies of *The Upper Room* or *Our Daily Bread*.

8. Make sure the new person is integrated into the communication system of the church by being added to the newsletter mailing list, the e-mail list, and on the prayer chain as that person is comfortable doing so.

9. If you develop an especially close bond with the guest or new member, invite that person to athletic events, concerts, or other activities that you can enjoy together. You may want to invite them to a weekend retreat if such events are offered by your church or denomination.

10. Find out birthdays and wedding anniversary (if married), and send them cards. If your church issues a monthly birthday and wedding anniversary calendar, make sure they are included.

11. Watch for any problems the person may be experiencing and offer assistance—calling on others to help as needed and notifying the pastor(s) immediately if there are problems or difficulties you cannot handle or would be better served by a pastor.

12. Let the coordinator of faith friends or coordinator of assimilation know how the journey is going for the guest or new member. Ask for help if needed.

Assimilation or Faith Friend Coordinator

The Faith Friend or Assimilation Coordinator matches faith friends with new people in the church. In a very small congregation, the pastor might choose to accept this coordinating role. In medium-sized and larger congregations, a volunteer is important. Ed Bontrager developed a form, which makes it easier to keep track of a new person's involvement in the congregation. That form begins on the next page and can be photocopied for use in your congregation. The assimilation coordinator or the faith friend can keep track of the information. If the faith friend keeps track of the information, updated information should be shared periodically with the assimilation coordinator.

Name _____

Phone _____

Address _____

_____

Email address _____

Family Members with approximate ages _____

_____

Occupation(s) _____

Date	**Occasion**
_____	First visit
_____	First Sunday school class attended
_____	Other activity
_____	Visit by pastor or other caller
_____	Name included on mailbox
_____	Name added to newsletter mailing list
_____	Attended a small group

Which small group? _____

_____ Became member of small group

_____ Involved in other peer group, e.g. choir, ball team, women's Bible study...

_____ Invited to attend membership class

_____ Completed membership class

Other involvements or responsibilities:

_____ _____

_____ _____

_____ _____

_____ _____

_____ Joined as a member

Top four spiritual gifts or talents:

_____

_____

_____

_____

Other observations or ideas shared:

_____

_____

A pastor or assimilation coordinator keeps a record of each new person and fills in the form as integrative factors take place. A larger congregation may need to have a single assimilation coordinator who works closely with multiple faith friend coordinators. In a large congregation, regular meetings of coordinators with church staff can help the communication process and can also help ensure that the needs of new people are being met.

The next page gives an example of an information sheet that the coordinator of assimilation or a faith friend can ask new people to complete. Another approach is to simply ask the questions and complete the sheet for the new person. The spiritual gifts process described in the next chapter is a valuable one to use with new people in the congregation.

Along with finding out what people prefer to do, finding out what they prefer not to do can help leaders avoid wasted time and unnecessary frustration in the early stages of new member assimilation. The items on the next page are adapted from a Member Preference Grid, published by Energize, Inc., 5450 Wissahickon Ave., Philadelphia, PA 19144.

Information Sheet

Skills/knowledge I have that I enjoy using _____

_____

Things I would like to get the chance to learn _____

_____

Things I hope I never get asked to do _____

_____

Skills/knowledge I'd rather use only occasionally _____

_____

Resources I have access to that I might be able to share _____

_____

When and where I prefer receiving calls, letters, or emails _____

_____

When and where I prefer not being contacted _____

_____

I would like to be considered for the following possible
opportunities in the church _____

_____

Ephesians and the Cost of Welcoming New People

Ephesians 2:19–22 tells us that since we are one in Christ we "are no longer strangers and aliens, you are citizens with the saints and also members of the household of God. . . ." [v. 19]. The question we face is how to help people who are seeking a new fellowship feel like members of the household of God rather than like strangers and aliens. William Barclay, commenting on these verses, tells about a man in a strange city:

> *He was lonely. He used to walk the streets at evening time; and sometimes through an uncurtained window he would see a family sitting around the table or the fire in happy fellowship. And then the curtain would be drawn and he would feel shut out, and lonely in the dark.*

Barclay goes on to say, "That is what cannot happen in the family of God. And that is what should never happen in the Church. Through Jesus there is a seat and a place for every one of us." [William Barclay, *The Letter to the Galatians and Ephesians,* Philadelphia: Westminster Press, 1958, pp. 138–139]

Ed admits that despite being a minister for many years, being at home in church settings, and knowing many people in his denomination, there are still times he walks into a new church and feels like an intruder or a foreigner. Imagine how a person feels who has never belonged to a church or who has not attended for many years!

This is where we come in—those of us already assimilated. How do we help the new person? The initial friendliness is extremely important. But what happens after that is even more significant. Our ability to truly incorporate the new person into congregational life will determine whether that person remains a stranger or becomes part of the family of God.

Assimilation does carry a price tag. It means making new friends, opening up our social networks, being willing to change some hallowed traditions, sharing leadership, adopting new programs, and cultivating openness to the ideas of new people. If the church is successful at outreach and assimilation, it may even mean expanding the physical facilities. We are the ones who determine whether or not someone becomes part of the family of God, remains a stranger, or simply leaves the church.

Membership Expectations

As guests begin to feel true acceptance in the congregation, they will begin to ask, "What does it mean to be a member of this church?" In many congregations it means attending one or more sessions of a membership class, followed by coming forward in a worship service to take vows of membership. This "easy entrance" approach is relatively common in congregations across North America.

This relatively low expectation approach may also contribute to the fact that so many people join congregations and then become inactive. That inactivity has multiple causes, including the reality that many churches stop worrying about assimilation once someone has become a member. But the low expectations don't encourage new members to take initiative themselves to become more integrated into congregational life

Church consultant Lyle Schaller contrasts low expectation congregations with high expectation congregations. High expectation congregations outline in advance attitudes and behaviors toward which new members should strive. These are also expectations that should apply to those who are already in the congregation!

The faith friend or the assimilation coordinator may want to monitor how new members are doing in meeting the expectations that have been shared with them. This shouldn't be monitoring in a legalistic or judgmental kind of way but the failure to meet these expectations should be viewed as a "warning light," indicating that further outreach to the new member is needed. Some expectations can be easily monitored by observing outward behavior, but there are others that are not visible to an outside observer. Here are some expectations based in part on Schaller's teaching and also on observation of high expectation congregations:

1. Daily prayer and Bible reading using a devotional resource like *The Upper Room* or *Our Daily Bread*.

2. Weekly participation in worship.

3. Being part of an adult study program like a Sunday school class, a Bible study group, or a Saturday morning prayer breakfast.

4. Serving as a volunteer in the life, ministry, and outreach of the congregation.

5. Regular financial support of the church and its outreach, with a tithe (10%) as the goal toward which people strive.

6. A willingness to share the faith with others and to invite others to church.

7. Becoming involved in a small task-oriented group like the choir or other music group, women's or men's organization, service project, or sports team.

8. A willingness to connect with others in the congregation and to be of help to people in need.

If a congregation moves to such high expectations of new members, it's important that existing members also be striving to meet those expectations. New members will quickly and also justifiably become resentful if the expectations don't apply to everyone.

And expectations in the Christian community should never be legalistic. The New Testament is clear about the reality that all of us fall short of living as Christ would have us live. The high expectations, however, are meaningful targets that urge us to deepen our involvement, growing closer to God and to others in the faith community.

Worship and Transformation

People who return to a church after many years, or try it out for the first time, come for a reason. When people come back to church they sometimes come because of a crisis experience in their lives. Their material success may not be fulfilling. They may have just gone through a divorce or be new parents. We attribute these famous words to Saint Augustine:

There is a God-sized hole in the heart of every person, and nothing will satisfy that except God.

And so finally, perhaps with trepidation, they decide to come to church. When they come they are seeking something to fill their hearts and lift their spirits.

Some churches, unfortunately, lack energy and vitality. Guests who come discover a worship experience that is not well planned, does not flow easily from one element to another, and has detached themes, uninspired singing, and a non-practical, dry sermon. Guests in congregations that have an open time for members to share their joys and concerns may find themselves listening to lengthy litanies of problems and to comments that are only understood by those who are already involved in the church.

Donald C. Posterski and Irwin Barker, Canadian church growth experts say, "Worship without creativity is like inviting a congregation to come and chew on Kleenex for an hour." They go on to say, "Christians today want a style of worship that is both meaningful and recognizable." [*Where's a Good Church?*, Winfield, BC: Woodlake Books, p. 27]

In his research, George Barna discovered that half the people sitting in worship services week-after-week have not experienced God's presence in the past year, and one-third have never experienced God's presence at all. Thus it would appear that many worship services are not transforming people who have been members for years, making it even less likely that they will transform guests!

In worship planning, pastors and worship committees need to keep in mind both those who are already members and those who might come as guests. Worship committees often benefit by having at least a couple of younger, more recent members of the church helping with the planning process.

People are seeking religious experiences that will transform their lives. The style of the service may differ significantly from one effective congregation to another, but there are some characteristics that are usually present:

• The worship service has high energy and enthusiasm.

• The quality of the music, whether traditional or contemporary, is high.

- The sermon speaks directly to the daily lives of people, giving them practical guidance on how to live and on how to deepen their faith.

- The prayers are in everyday language and speak to the deepest needs of people.

- The welcome from others at the service is warm and genuine, not smothering or manipulative.

People who have not grown up in the church may not know the meaning of words like grace, original sin, or salvation. They may not be familiar with the parable of the Prodigal Son or the full story of Moses and the Exodus. They probably will not know that the book of Genesis contains not one but two stories of creation. Both in worship and in Christian education settings, it's important not to "assume" knowledge on the part of new people and not to make them feel ignorant or unwelcome because they do not know things that others take for granted.

The worship service and the interactions with the people of the congregation should have transforming impact on people who have never been part of a church or who have not been part of a church for many years. Consider these comments from people about the way that their lives have been changed by new or renewed contact with a congregation:

From a forty-year-old woman: "The death of my mother was just devastating. She was only sixty-one years old, and my father and all of us had just assumed she would be around for another two or three decades. All of us were crushed, including my husband and our two children. The minister was very kind, and some of his words privately and in the memorial service made me consider the possibility that I had been missing something by having been out of the church for such a long time. My husband had no interest in worship, but I started attending a church a few blocks away from our home. The minister there had these practical, easy-to-understand sermons that started helping me in renewing my spiritual life.

"Then this wonderful woman from the congregation reached out to me and invited me to have lunch with her. She'd lost her own mother a few years earlier, and she really understood what I was feeling. I found myself crying in the restaurant and not even caring that other people gave me these strange looks. This woman had such a strong faith, and she really helped me believe that God would see me through the pain.

"As I found myself changing, I wanted the same thing for my husband and children. It wasn't hard to get the kids started at the mid-week study night at the church and going with me on Sunday morning. My husband was another matter. It took a long time, but eventually he started going with me as well. All of us have just been so blessed with God's presence in our lives."

From a thirty-three-year-old man: "I've stayed away from the church my whole adult life, ever sense I discovered that I was gay. I'm African-American, and most black churches are horribly negative on homosexuality. I just decided not to go where I wasn't wanted. Then I had this really good friend who ended up dying of AIDS, and I was just amazed that he kept going to church right up to the end. He was always telling me that he was praying for me and that he wanted me to pray for him. I wasn't even sure that I still believed in God, but I wanted to honor his request. So it was like I started praying not sure I believed and someplace along the way I started to believe.

"After his death, there was this memorial service at his church that was so filled with life and with hope. It was a largely African-American congregation, but the preacher said nothing negative about my friend's homosexuality. He talked about God's acceptance of everyone, and I felt myself feeling really hungry for that kind of acceptance. I started attending worship at that church. There were these wonderful people who reached out to me and made me feel so welcome. Church started to become the high point of my life, and I was looking forward to what I would hear and learn. Christ really came alive in my heart."

From a fifty-three-year-old woman: "I've never had any use for the church, and I've really resented the religious people who've felt like they needed to convert me. I mean, I've seen how some of those so-called religious people treat others; and if that's what faith does for you, I wanted no part of it. But I got talked into joining a quilting group that meets in a church. I knew two of the women in it, and they promised me that no one would pressure me to talk about religion or go to church.

"I found out that in addition to working on their own quilting projects, some of the women in the church made quilts to give to people who were in the hospital or the nursing home or who were shut-ins. I thought that was a nice thing to do, so I started helping with it. Then I went along on deliveries of a couple of those quilts, and I was moved myself by how much it meant to those who received them.

"And I started to see that the people in this quilting group, for the most part, were religious without being obnoxious or pushy. These people were the real thing. I started going to worship at the church because I was curious about what was happening. That just changed my life. The worship service was so moving, and I started to understand that this wasn't about me as an individual but it was about all of us as the children of God. And I started to get the message that there was a God who really did love me and who had actually been watching out for me my whole life, waiting for me to open my heart. Things were never the same for me again."

In most instances, people's lives are changed and people become fully assimilated because of a combination of the transforming experiences they have in a congregation and because of the outreach and the caring of others in the congregation.

Sharing Leadership

One church growth writer tells the following story. "In a conversation with the pastor of church in the Pacific Northwest, I asked the question, 'How long would I need to be a member of your church before I might be elected to the board?' He considered my question for a moment and then asked, 'Would you attend regularly, give faithfully, and exemplify the Christian life?' 'Yes,' I responded. 'Then you would likely be elected to the board of this church sometime between the twelfth and fourteenth year after you joined.'"

The writer goes on to say, "No wonder this church had been in decline for the past generation. It has a terminal illness.... Unfortunately, too often power in the church is closely protected by the 'old guard.' Newcomers are seen as liabilities rather than as assets. Their ideas are dismissed as inappropriate or ill-conceived. They are excluded from informal decision-making conversations, and their new ideas never get a serious hearing."

This illustration introduces the price tag of bringing new people into leadership to help make major decisions for the church—both its present and future. Why do older members guard those posts? First, serving on a board or church council gives them status. Second, making sure long-term members retain these positions keeps unorthodox and new ideas from being implemented, thus keeping ecclesiastical life from going down the "wrong track," according to their belief.

However, the perceived "wrong track" is more than likely the "right track" if the church wants to assimilate people and help its members really live out the Great Commission.

It's crucial to involve in church leadership persons who have joined within the last two or three years. We do have to be careful not to push new members too hard and scare them off. We can give them too much responsibility too soon and create a situation where they fail. That is detrimental to the new member as well as the church.

But most congregations more often move too slowly in giving newer members positions of leadership and thus squander a valuable resource, by discouraging one's use of his or her spiritual gifts. Sometimes giving people opportunity to be a team teacher or a member of a board or committee can be valuable preparation for their being a lead teacher or a board or committee chairperson. It depends on the spiritual gifts and the temperament of the person. Having newer members involved in leadership brings several benefits to the congregation:

1. New members are enthusiastic about the pastor. Generally the pastor is a strong influence who helps keep new members coming back. As a result, they support the leadership of the pastor, enjoy her or his preaching, and deeply respect his or her opinion. They are a good witness for the church because they speak highly of the pastor. Newer members are especially helpful in pastoral evaluations. If a church faces a pastoral change, at least one person who has been a part of the church for two years or less should be on the search committee.

2. New members are very positive about the future of the church. The church met many of their perceived needs, or they would not have joined. They have built relationships with other newer members and with long-time members. Their enthusiasm will be contagious.

3. New members are open to innovation and new ideas. If realizing future possibilities in the church requires change in the present, new members will vote "yes" almost every time. By contrast, long-time members often tend to be past-oriented and more committed to perpetuating the status quo. Lyle Schaller has said, "The constant infusion of new Christians into our fellowship is required to keep alive the spiritual vitality which characterized the early church."

Ed had a new member in a congregation he pastored who was quickly responsible for an attractive new sign for the church and for a video projector for use in worship. Ed had been frustrated for some time by the old run-down, discolored sign, with broken bricks, that older members felt was good enough. The new member even generously absorbed most of the cost of the video projector.

4. New members are not as attached to the present location or facilities. A church that grows will eventually be reviewing its space. New members are far more likely to support a change of location, if need be, or the refurbishing of present facilities. A structure that has served a congregation for many years may possess certain portions of the edifice that are sacred to the longtime members. This could include such things as stained glass windows or even whole rooms donated in memory of loved ones. These memorial items can hinder forward move-ment. Newer members can be instrumental in moving the church into the future. People can work together to identify creative ways to integrate these family heirlooms into the new structure.

Over the years congregations keep gathering up more and more traditions, like barnacles on a ship lost at sea. Traditions keep growing. Churches bound by tradition may consider the following questions when trying to plan for the future: "How did we do it before?" "It's been working for 30 years. Why change it now?" "Let's think about it until next year's annual meeting and bring it up then." Change-resisting excuses like "We never did it that way before" or "I think we'd better stick to the same budget we had last year" are death knells for the church. Assimilating new persons and allowing them into leadership will be one way to maintain a forward look and bring about revitalization and growth.

Important Ratios for the Growing Church

These ratios can be helpful guidelines in thinking about how to position a church for growth and health. They may not be realistic in every situation, but your congregation will benefit by taking them seriously.

60:100—There should be 60 **tasks or roles** for every 100 members.

7:100—There should be seven **small groups** or units for every 100 members.

1:6—One out of six groups should have **started in the last two years** (churches that grow by 8–10% per year need to develop groups more rapidly).

1:7—When a new person begins attending church, seven **friendships** among the membership should be formed within the first six months.

1:5—One out of five of the **board members** should have joined within the last one to four years.

5:10—Five out of ten **first-time visitors** should be involved in some way within a year. If this isn't happening, then look carefully at how assimilation is being done.

10:10—Ten out of ten **new members** should still be actively involved a year after joining.

1:150—There should be one **full-time staff member** for every 150 people in worship.

The spiritual gifts assessment process shared in the next chapter originally appeared in the book Preaching, Planning, and Plumbing *by Steve Clapp, Ron Finney, and Angela Zizak. The process has been used in thousands of congregations in North America and has been refined since its first publication.*

Chapter Five
Spiritual Gifts and the Church

1 Corinthians 12

Concept: When people know their spiritual gifts, their connection to Christ and the church can be deepened. When the church utilizes the spiritual gifts of all people, the ministry of the church becomes wider.

Bill was at first annoyed when his pastor asked everyone in the congregation to complete a spiritual gifts assessment form. Bill thought that he already knew his abilities and talents, and responding to the questions felt like a waste of time. But Bill wanted to be cooperative with the pastor, so he completed the form and then asked his wife to complete the same form, sharing her opinions about Bill's gifts.

The results confirmed some of Bill's self-assessments. He ranked high on the gifts of administration and leadership, as he had felt sure he would. Both his professional work and his volunteer service to the church involved the use of those gifts. The spiritual gifts process, however, also included a surprise for Bill. In addition to ranking high on administration and leadership, Bill also ranked high on the gifts of counseling and encouragement. He had more people-helping skills than he had realized. When he talked with his pastor about the results, his pastor suggested that perhaps Bill's gifts of counseling and encouragement were part of the reason he was so successful as a leader. Bill also began to identify new possibilities for helping the people in the church and at his place of work. The possibility that God had given him these gifts made him feel a need to more fully explore them.

Joyce was delighted when her orientation to membership in the church included the completion of a spiritual gifts inventory. She had never considered the possibility that God had actually given her specific gifts to be used in the service of the church and also to be used in ministry beyond the programs of the church. She had often felt that she could be a good teacher, but she had lacked the self-confidence to do any volunteer work as a teacher in her previous church home. When the spiritual gifts inventory confirmed that she had the gift of teaching, she decided to take that seriously. She signed up for the teacher orientation program of the church and volunteered to help with an elementary Sunday school class. The congregation had a great need for more teachers, and she found herself welcomed into the orientation and then the class with great enthusiasm from others working with the educational program. Both she and the church were enriched.

Andrea had been the chairperson of the Property Commission in her church for six years. While she thought that she did a capable job in that position, she never enjoyed the meetings that she had to chair or all the details that she had to keep straight. When she completed a spiritual gifts assessment, she discovered that administration and leadership were not her strongest spiritual gifts. She came out strongest on evangelism. As she thought about the spiritual gifts results, she realized that she was always excited when she had the opportunity to tell someone else about her faith and about her church. And the church almost desperately needed more people to be reaching out to people in the community. Andrea decided to finish out her current term on the Property Commission and then to shift the focus of her work to more direct evangelism.

Her enthusiasm for evangelism was contagious. She not only succeeded in bringing new people into the church herself but also encouraged others she knew in the congregation to do more outreach.

One of the best ways for people to be thoroughly assimilated into the life of a congregation is for them to discover their spiritual gifts and find opportunities to utilize them in the church. While this can be especially powerful for persons like Joyce who are new to the congregation, it can also be a means for the revitalization and sometimes the deeper assimilation of longer-term members of the church as was the case for Andrea and Bill.

If you have not gone through a spiritual gifts assessment or discernment process yourself, we encourage you to complete the exercise in this chapter for your own benefit. We also encourage you to build a spiritual gifts process into the life of the congregation and to include that process as part of the orientation of new people.

Spiritual Gifts Overview

The Protestant tradition affirms not only the concept of the priesthood of all believers but also the belief that God has given us gifts to be used in service to the church and to others. Some people think of spiritual gifts narrowly like speaking in tongues or having the gift of healing, but most spiritual gifts are not spectacular or controversial.

An understanding of your spiritual gifts can be a significant help in focusing what you do not only within the church but also in your daily life. Most of us have between two and five spiritual gifts, and we should seek to maximize those gifts in our ministries and in our lives. That doesn't mean, of course, that we only work within the areas of our spiritual gifts. Every local church has numerous important tasks that must be done— whether someone feels gifted in each of those areas or not! To the extent that it is possible, however, people are more fulfilled and energized when they work in their areas of giftedness. That reality is true of laypersons in the church and also true of clergy. It's also true for those working in secular settings.

Spiritual gifts are not:

- acquired skills or natural abilities. Such skills and abilities are often used in the practice of spiritual gifts but are not the same thing. Cooking and cleaning, for example, are not themselves spiritual gifts but may help with the gift of hospitality.

- roles or offices (like being a pastor or the church treasurer).

- related only to the health and work of the church as an organization. We are part of the ministry of the overall body of Christ, which means that our gifts are to be used not only in relationship to the church as an organization but also in our homes, in our neighborhoods, and at places of secular employment.

- intended to be used for self-glory or in a way that divides the body of Christ. Spiritual gifts need to be held with true humility and thankfulness. The fact that one is especially gifted in an area does not mean that no one else should work in that area or that the opinions of others should not be respected.

- the same for everyone. Different people have different gifts. That's how the body of Christ works. No one person has all the gifts needed but by working together people find that the overall needs of the church can be met. There may be times, however, when a church in decline is missing some gifts which would be helpful.

> **Read chapter twelve in First Corinthians
> for a better understanding of the role
> that each person plays in the healthy
> functioning of the body of Christ.**

- an excuse for neglecting areas of need. We should all practice acts of encouragement, for example, even though some are especially gifted in that area. All of us need to reach out to others, inviting them to be part of the Christian community, even if we do not personally possess the gift of evangelism.

- ***necessarily clearly revealed by any system of human design, including this one.*** Assessment systems can, however, be a significant aid to you in better understanding your spiritual gifts.

Spiritual gifts are:

- unmerited favors or gifts from God. We do not earn them or receive them as rewards for what we have done.

- an indicator of areas in which we should be working in the life of the church and in our daily lives as well.

- able to be more fully developed by study and practice. A person with the gift of teaching, for example, will be a better teacher with training and careful preparation.

- meant to be used as part of the body of Christ—so that we work together in mutually beneficial ways not only in the institutional church but also in society as a whole.

- confirmed to us through prayer and through the feedback of the Christian community. We recommend, for example, that you have at least one other person complete an assessment form *about you* in addition to the one you complete. Seeing how another person experiences or observes your gifts will help in the assessment process.

As already indicated, there are many different systems for assessing spiritual gifts. The gifts described here are similar to those in several other spiritual gift assessment systems. They are organized here into three major categories:

1. Communication Gifts
2. Organization-strengthening Gifts
3. Relationship Gifts

The spiritual gifts of speaking in tongues and of healing are less commonly found and are not able to be assessed by a system such as this one. The gifts of tongues and of healing can be of value to the body of Christ when used in a supportive way, but they can also be divisive, especially when too much importance is placed on them.

Four Communication Gifts

Prophecy: The God-given ability to share and interpret God's message and call to justice for the repentance, enrichment, or uplifting of the body of Christ and of persons and organizations outside of the church. This may be communicated through the written or the spoken word. Note that one may have the gift of prophecy without necessarily being an extremely skilled preacher. It's also possible to be a skilled preacher as a manifestation of the gift of teaching without having the gift of prophecy. Some persons express the gift of prophecy in speaking directly to secular organizations or to society as a whole. Some large corporations have prophets in their midst who become a kind of "corporate conscience" which may make a tremendous difference in those organizations.

Teaching: The God-given ability to teach others how to understand Scripture, God, relationships, themselves, and the world in which we have been placed. While we especially think of this gift being utilized in the educational program and ministry of the church, it also finds expression in quality preaching. Those with the gift of teaching may also employ it in significant ways in secular school systems or anywhere there is opportunity to help others learn. In secular settings, of course, one must respect the diversity of beliefs and not impose the faith on others.

Artistic Expression: The God-given ability to share God's love through one or more art forms such as music, drama, poetry, painting, sculpturing, etc. We find evidence of people having this gift throughout the Old and the New Testaments. The expression of this gift is not limited to the life of the church as an organization.

Intercession: The God-given ability to live a life much of which is immersed in prayer for the needs of other people, the church, and the world. The communication is between the person and God, though it may become public in services of worship and other settings.

Four Organization-Strengthening Gifts

Administration: The God-given ability to understand organizations and to further the work of the body of Christ through efficiency, planning, and procedure. This gift is a great blessing to those with management responsibilities. While we especially think of the expression of this gift within the church, persons in secular employment may see administrative functions as an expression of a God-given gift, to be used for the sharing of God's love.

Craftsmanship: The God-given ability to create resources needed in the body of Christ (which can include carpentry, sewing, etc.). People who are gifted in this area may also find great meaning in secular work that involves a high level of creativity in construction and design.

Generosity: The God-given ability to contribute money and material resources to the work of the body of Christ with a thankful heart. The fact that one has this gift does not automatically mean that one is wealthy, and the fact that one is wealthy does not mean that one necessarily possesses this gift. The work of the body of Christ is done not only through the institutional church but also through secular organizations, so support of worthy causes outside the church may also be an expression of this spiritual gift. People with this gift often have a high ability to cultivate generosity in others. (The fact that some are especially gifted in this area does not mean that others have no obligation to be generous! The tithe stands as a realistic goal for all Christians.)

Service: The God-given ability to experience spiritual value in practical tasks which support the work of the church and help others. This is closely related to the gift of hospitality. People with this gift may also find great meaning in the service they offer at secular work and in community organizations.

Five Relationship Gifts

Counseling: The God-given ability to effectively listen to people and guide them in becoming more fulfilled spiritually, psychologically, and socially. People who are gifted in this area can find many opportunities to utilize and develop the gift in secular work as well as in the life of the church.

Encouragement: The God-given ability to support, encourage, and strengthen those who are suffering or who are going through a crisis in their faith or in their lives. As with counseling, there are many opportunities in the secular world to utilize this gift—in the home, in neighborhoods, in volunteer work, and in secular employment.

Evangelism: The God-given ability to share Christ's message with people who have no faith or who are unsure of their faith—so that they can move toward deeper relationships with Christ. While possessing this gift can obviously be a tremendous advantage for a pastor, there are many with the gift who choose to work in secular occupations because of the opportunities for involvement with people which those occupations bring. (Again, remember that the fact some are especially gifted in this area does not change the obligation of all people to share their faith.)

Hospitality: The God-given ability to embrace people, including strangers, and to provide companionship, food, and shelter when needed. This is related to but not identical with the kind of biblical hospitality which we are all obligated to practice as part of the body of Christ. Many people with this gift find meaning working in the social services field or doing volunteer work with nonprofits which serve the homeless, the hungry, and the imprisoned.

Leadership: The God-given ability to identify and communicate a vision or mission and to direct people in making the vision or mission a reality. This is not the same as the gift of administration. The gift of leadership is very powerful and can be utilized in a wide range of occupations as well as in the church.

The Bible on Spiritual Gifts

As you are preparing to work through the spiritual gifts assessment process that follows, you may find it helpful to read some of the biblical references to spiritual gifts. For example:

- 1 Corinthians 12–14
- Romans 12
- Ephesians 4
- 1 Peter 4
- James 5:14–16 and 1 Timothy 2:1–2 (intercession)
- Other references to artistic expression and to craftsmanship are found in many Old Testament passages.

Variations in Spiritual Gifts Identified

Some systems of spiritual gifts take just one of the biblical passages shared above as a standard and include only those gifts which are explicitly named in that passage. Others broaden the concept considerably and may include as spiritual gifts celibacy, exorcism, and martyrdom. There do not seem to be many people eager to claim those gifts in our time!

While spiritual gifts are divine blessings, all systems of identifying and assessing spiritual gifts, as already mentioned, are human systems—with all the shortcomings that accompany everything else we do as human beings! The gifts included in the following inventory reflect the gifts identified by a substantial number of persons who have studied this field. The system is biblical, but it does include some contemporary terminology (such as "counseling" for those gifted at helping people in their quest for wholeness). There may well be spiritual gifts which are not reflected as such in Scripture or in any inventory system. Some people feel that "parenting" or "child raising" is a spiritual gift even though all of us who parent learn to cultivate our skills in that area.

Inventories like this one, the feedback of people who know you very well, and group discussions can be a help in clarifying gifts. The bottom line is that each person must prayerfully consider what spiritual gifts he or she has and how those should be used.

Completing the Assessments

You may wish to make one or more photocopies of the assessment that follows so that you can ask at least one friend or family member to complete it for you. Then you can compare those responses to your own.

It's best not to reflect at great length on the answers to individual items in the assessment. Simply move through, giving your first inclination as a response in most instances.

When completed, transfer the numerical responses to the overview or summary sheet that follows the assessment items. By totaling those in the indicated columns, you'll have weighted responses on the thirteen spiritual gifts. The three or four highest scores are most likely spiritual gifts for you. Some people, however, may find only one or two which clearly stand out from the others in terms of score; and some may find as many as six or seven which have high scores.

Have at least one person who knows you extremely well complete the items for you, and transfer the numerical scores to the overview or summary sheet provided. Obviously there are some items that require the friend or associate to make educated estimates concerning your impact on other people or how you feel about certain experiences. Those estimates, however, reflect something of how you come across to others and are valuable feedback.

It's important that you clearly communicate to anyone who completes the assessment for you that you want that person's honest feedback. Ideal persons to complete the form for you would include a spouse, a person at your place of work who has known you for two or more years, a person who has been a friend for many years, or an active lay person or staff member in the church who has worked with you for two or more years. You may decide to have three or four people complete the assessment for you. Make as many copies as you need for that purpose.

Compare the results of the assessment of other persons with your own. Where the assessments are essentially in agreement, you have added confirmation of the validity of those spiritual gifts. If there are spiritual gifts where you and a person doing the friend or associate assessment are not in agreement, you want to put the final confidence in your own assessment. The fact that you are not in agreement, however, may cause you to look again at your own responses to the items used to produce the weighted score for that spiritual gift (simply follow the numbers in the column on the overview sheet for that gift). You might determine that your initial responses were too high or too low based on the additional feedback.

As you reflect and pray on the assessment results, you may decide that you have a spiritual gift that did not emerge as a result of the inventory process. You may also be surprised by a spiritual gift that emerged. If either of those is the case, visit about the results with someone who knows you well. You may decide that you do have a spiritual gift that needs further development. You may decide that something you had thought was a spiritual gift may not actually be so. And you may decide that the assessment process was simply wrong at a particular point. In the end, you want to trust your own reflection and prayer rather than this or any other assessment process.

Spiritual Gifts Assessment

Respond to each statement which follows using this numerical system:

5	=	This is highly descriptive of me virtually all of the time.
4	=	This is descriptive of me most of the time.
3	=	This is descriptive of me some of the time.
2	=	This is descriptive of me only rarely.
1	=	This is not descriptive of me.

It is very important for you to respond to these statements in terms of how you actually are rather than in terms of how you feel you should be. Don't be shy about acknowledging strengths, and don't feel badly because some statements are not descriptive of you. There are no "right" or "wrong" answers—only honest responses.

Don't spend too much time thinking about a particular item. Go with your first impression, or leave the item blank and return to it later.

_____ 1. I am able to convey ideas and insights in a way that motivates people to want to learn more.

_____ 2. I speak the truth about what I feel is right even when that is unpopular and hard for other people to accept.

_____ 3. I am willing to accept responsibility for organizations or groups that lack a clear sense of direction or leadership and seek to help them change.

_____ 4. In the midst of other activities, I find myself focusing on the needs of another person and praying for that individual.

_____ 5. I feel that an important purpose of my home is to be a place to care for others, including people who are not part of my family.

_____ 6. I find satisfaction in working behind the scenes to help others make the most of their gifts and abilities.

_____ 7. I find pleasure in sharing my material resources with persons in need.

_____ 8. I cultivate relationships with persons who do not know Christ so that I can lead them to Him.

_____ 9. I can empathize with people who are going through difficult times and find meaning in involving myself in their healing processes.

_____ 10. I enjoy developing my skills in communicating through music, drama, or other art forms.

_____ 11. I am fulfilled when I am able to build or create something that helps the church or other people.

_____ 12. I am able to recognize what people truly want to communicate both from what they say and from what they do not say.

_____ 13. I find pleasure in learning about how organizations function.

_____ 14. People say they learn a lot from my teaching, and they seem motivated to want to learn more on their own.

_____ 15. I am willing to accept personal suffering and criticism if it will result in myself and others growing closer to God or doing the right thing by God's standards.

_____ 16. I've given leadership to groups that have sensed God's presence or gained a sense of purpose even in the middle of difficult times.

_____ 17. A day does not seem complete to me unless I have spent time praying for the needs of other individuals, of the church, and of the world.

_____ 18. I enjoy doing all that I can to help new people feel that they belong.

_____ 19. I like to encourage others by serving wherever and whenever there is a need.

_____ 20. I find significant meaning in knowing my financial support makes a difference in the ministries of the church or of another service organization.

_____ 21. After I lead people to a closer relationship with God, I guide them into deeper discipleship and service.

_____ 22. I find meaning in motivating others to have more concern about the health of their souls.

_____ 23. I can communicate my sense of God more through music or other artistic means than through conversation.

_____ 24. I can fashion raw materials into finished objects.

_____ 25. I can continue to maintain a positive relationship with people even when it's necessary to express substantial disagreement or to raise questions about what they're doing.

_____ 26. I can grasp the overall purpose or goals of an organization or group and work out plans for accomplishing them.

_____ 27. I can draw other people into considering how their relationships with God or a sense of meaning and purpose should affect their daily lives.

_____ 28. Even in the face of criticism or pressure, I challenge people to examine their lives and change their direction when needed.

_____ 29. I can decisively manage people and resources in positive ways to bring a vision or mission into reality.

_____ 30. The names of people who are especially in need of God's help are never far from my mind.

_____ 31. I enjoy providing food and lodging for people in need.

_____ 32. I like to use my natural and my learned skills to enable the work of others.

_____ 33. When I know that someone else is in need of resources that I have, I don't worry about replenishing what I give.

_____ 34. When I tell others what God has done in my life, they respond with renewed faith of their own.

_____ 35. I can motivate others to take their faith more seriously in their lives.

_____ 36. People accuse me of being temperamental like an artist.

_____ 37. I feel that I honor God with things I make by hand.

_____ 38. I can empathize with and help people who are resentful, angry, or confused.

_____ 39. I have skill in coordinating the gifts of people for greater effectiveness.

_____ 40. I love to help others gain greater skill in understanding and expressing themselves.

_____ 41. I can motivate others to use their faith in making decisions in both their private and their public lives.

_____ 42. I usually have a clear sense of what needs to be done in an organization and can motivate others in that direction.

_____ 43. People frequently express appreciation to me for my having continued to remember them in my prayers.

_____ 44. I readily reach out to persons needing physical or emotional encouragement.

_____ 45. When I see a wide range of needs, I want to help with as many as I can.

_____ 46. I have been successful at earning or discovering significant amounts of money for the Lord's work.

_____ 47. I want people around me to know I am a Christian and hope that may provide opportunities to help them draw closer to Christ.

_____ 48. I am able to strengthen people who are wavering in their sense of purpose in life.

_____ 49. Through my artistic expressions, people have gained deeper insights into themselves or into the spiritual life.

_____ 50. I can design and build things to help the church or other organizations better serve people.

_____ 51. I show my concern by helping people find practical solutions to spiritual, relational, or personal struggles.

_____ 52. I like to improve the efficiency of organizations with which I work.

_____ 53. I enjoy finding practical guidance in the Bible and sharing that help with others.

_____ 54. I feel compelled to confront people when they display behaviors or attitudes which are destructive.

_____ 55. I can enthusiastically organize people to achieve goals which I feel are important.

_____ 56. I have had times when I was so absorbed in my prayers for the needs of others that I lost all track of time.

_____ 57. I like to help new people get acquainted with others in the church and in other settings.

_____ 58. I believe there is spiritual significance in the routine tasks I do for others.

_____ 59. Because I want to see significant things happen in ministry, I give more than a tithe (over 10%).

_____ 60. I continually seek to find different or better ways to share my faith with others.

_____ 61. I enjoy reaching out to people in settings like hospitals, nursing homes, or prisons.

_____ 62. I like the challenge of communicating with variety and creativity.

_____ 63. I can visualize how something should be constructed before I build it.

_____ 64. People tell me that my patient and understanding listening helps them clarify their thoughts.

_____ 65. Once I know what the goal is, I have skill at developing the strategy to meet it.

_____ 66. I always find myself learning as I have opportunity to teach others.

_____ 67. I have had times when a concern was so heavy on my heart that I had to speak out no matter what the price.

_____ 68. Others seek me out to give leadership to various causes or organizations.

_____ 69. When I am deep into prayer for others, I often find myself communicating in images or feelings more than in words.

_____ 70. I feel that entertaining others in my home, at the church, or in other settings is one of the best ways that I am personally able to nurture genuine community.

_____ 71. I enjoy doing a variety of odd jobs around the church or other organizations to help meet the needs of people.

_____ 72. I am able to motivate others to financially support worthy causes.

_____ 73. I have the patience to work with another person over a long period of time in order to eventually bring that individual to faith in Christ.

_____ 74. I find great meaning in reaching out to persons at their times of greatest need no matter what the problem.

_____ 75. I enjoy developing my skills in the arts through music, crafts, drama, or other media.

_____ 76. I am gifted at putting things together and making them work.

_____ 77. I can generally help people see their problems from a new perspective and work toward a solution that is right for them.

_____ 78. I am good at and find pleasure in organizing many kinds of projects.

_____ 79. On the whole, I would rather teach a class or group than simply be a spectator.

_____ 80. I can confront people with problems in their own lives, in the church, or in society in a way that causes them to rethink their positions rather than simply be angry.

_____ 81. I can lead others through the development of a vision for their work together.

_____ 82. Praying for others several times a day feels almost as natural to me as breathing.

_____ 83. I feel a true calling to help new people become fully integrated into the life of the church or other organizations.

_____ 84. While I am often not the one giving direct leadership, a great many things in the organizations to which I belong would not get done without my willingness to do what is needed.

_____ 85. I give generously to God's work and genuinely do not seek or want any recognition or reward for what I do.

_____ 86. I feel that God often brings me into contact with people who need to discover or to rediscover Christ.

_____ 87. When people are going through difficult times, I am able to encourage them to maintain their faith and to do all they can to respond positively to the problems they face.

_____ 88. I feel that I have been especially gifted in terms of music, drama, painting, or another art form.

_____ 89. I have the ability to build or make things which will facilitate the work of the church or of other service organizations.

_____ 90. I am able to help people face the truth about themselves and their relationships with others when necessary to help them work through their problems.

_____   91. I am generally known as an efficient person who keeps track of things and follows through well.

When you've completed all 91 assessment items, transfer your scores to the chart which appears on this and the following page. Add each line across, producing a total on the left-hand side.

Teaching   1___   14___ 27___ 40___ 53___ 66___ 79___
Total___

Prophecy   2___   15___ 28___ 41___ 54___ 67___ 80___
Total___

Leadership   3___   16___ 29___ 42___ 55___ 68___ 81___
Total___

Intercession   4___   17___ 30___ 43___ 56___ 69___ 82___
Total___

Hospitality   5___   18___31___ 44___ 57___ 70___ 83___
Total___

Helps/Service 6___ 19___ 32___ 45___ 58___ 71___ 84___
Total___

Generosity   7___   20___ 33___ 46___ 59___ 72___ 85___
Total___

Evangelism   8___   21___ 34___ 47___ 60___ 73___ 86___
Total___

Encouragement 9___ 22___ 35___ 48___ 61___ 74___ 87___
Total___

Artistic Express. 10___ 23___ 36___ 49___62___75___ 88___
Total___

Craftsmanship 11___ 24___ 37___ 50___ 63___ 76___ 89___
Total___

Counseling   12___ 25___ 38___ 51___ 64___ 77___ 90___
Total___

Administration 13___ 26___ 39___ 52___ 65___ 78___ 91___
Total___

If you invited one or more others to complete the assessment for you, compare their scores with your own. If there are significant discrepancies, talk about those with the person or persons who completed the assessment for you. Be open to what they have to say, but ultimately have confidence in your own perceptions.

Now transfer your four highest scores to the following chart. Add your own comments about each spiritual gift that is listed. Consider these questions:

- Are there any surprises? If so, what are they?
- To what extent are the results what you expected? Are you pleased with the results? Disappointed with the results?
- Do you have additional scores that are almost as high as the fourth one you listed on the chart? If so, it is possible that those might also represent spiritual gifts.

Four Gifts with Highest Scores

1.   Gift: _____ Score: _____
Comment: _____

_____

2.   Gift: _____ Score: _____
Comment: _____

_____

3.   Gift: _____ Score: _____
Comment: _____

_____

4.   Gift: _____ Score: _____
Comment: _____

_____

**Some Common Observations
About the Spiritual Gifts Assessment**

1.   I only have one or two clear spiritual gifts by this system.   My other scores are all much lower.   Don't be concerned.   Some persons only have one or two spiritual gifts as measured by this kind of system.   What's important is thinking about the gifts that you have and developing them as effectively as possible.   (Occasionally a person will be uncomfortable responding to items in positive ways and will end up with scores that are artificially low.   You may want to try completing the assessment again, this time thinking more positively about yourself!)

2.   I really have seven or eight spiritual gifts that all have very high scores.   Then you are probably blessed with an above average number of spiritual gifts. This isn't a matter for pride since gifts come to us from God rather than from our own effort, but it does mean that you may have many opportunities to be of help to others.

3. I know that I have skills and abilities in an area in which I had a very low score on the assessment. Remember that spiritual gifts are not the same as skills and abilities. You may be doing excellent work in an area that isn't really one of spiritual giftedness for you. On the other hand, it's also possible that the problem is with the assessment instrument itself. This is not a perfect system! Think about it, pray about it, and visit with others about it.

4. I am almost shocked by how high my score was on one or two of the items. I really didn't think of myself as being gifted in those areas. It's always possible that the assessment process is at fault; but generally you should take very seriously any new areas of giftedness which emerge from this process. You may find that you'll have wonderful opportunities to develop the gift or gifts and that new directions will open for you.

5. I feel as though I am very gifted in work with computers and the Internet, but that doesn't seem to surface on this spiritual gifts assessment. Computers and the Internet provide wonderful opportunities for ministry and are, for the most part, significant blessings to our lives. They are, however, tools rather than gifts, just as curriculum is a tool for a teacher and paint and brushes tools for an artist or for a craftsperson. Thus various spiritual gifts may find expression through your use of computers and the Internet.

Spiritual Gifts and Assimilation

As shared near the beginning of this chapter, a spiritual gifts process can play an important role in the assimilation of people into your congregation. When people identify their spiritual gifts and the church recognizes those gifts, it becomes much easier to find the connecting points in the life of the congregation. Here are some suggestions to consider:

- If your church has not been using a spiritual gifts process, consider having everyone in the church complete a spiritual gifts assessment. Obviously the authors of this book would be happy for you to provide copies of the book to all adults in the church, and a church-wide study of the book will make a significant difference in your ability to assimilate new people. But if you aren't ready for such a study and want to utilize the spiritual gifts process, go to our website, www.churchstuff.com, to download the forms.

- Work with the personnel committee, nominating committee, calling and discernment committee, or other group in your church that is charged with helping match people to the volunteer needs of the church. Encourage them to begin utilizing the results of the spiritual gifts assessment as a guide in matching people to the needs of the congregation. You may wish to create a position of Spiritual Gifts Coordinator to help people in your church better understand and utilize their spiritual gifts.

- When new people join the congregation, have them complete a spiritual gifts assessment as a part of the orientation process. Then have the Spiritual Gifts Coordinator or another volunteer visit with each new member about the ways they may best be able to use their spiritual gifts in the life of the church.

- Be especially alert for new members and long-time members with the gifts of evangelism and hospitality. Those persons may well be able to have significant impact on your church's outreach efforts. Also remember, however, that evangelism and hospitality are part of the responsibility of all Christians, not just of those who are especially gifted in those areas.

Chapter Six
Children, Youth, and Young Adults

Matthew 19:13–15

Concept: Virtually all churches talk about the importance of having children, youth, and young adults involved, but we need to become more intentional about truly assimilating people of these ages into congregational life.

Having children in church is important to us, but I think they should be made to behave. When we have the children's story in the worship service, some of them just go running down the aisle. Their parents should teach them to walk.

When the teenagers in our church did the service on Youth Sunday, I just could not believe how they looked. I'm quite accustomed to long hair on young people. We've had that for generations. But they were wearing these t-shirts and shorts and flip-flops. And this one young man who read the Bible had this piercing right below his lip and three earrings in one ear. They should not be permitted to lead worship looking like that.

One of the young men who grew up in our church has come back after college. At first, I was so pleased that his girlfriend was coming to church with him. Then I learned that the two of them are living together and were the last year of college too. They not only are not married, they aren't even engaged. Some people have thought about putting him on the church board, and I am absolutely opposed to that.

> *We had two young men attend here for a while, and it was clear to us that they were gay. One of them had an absolutely wonderful singing voice and was a great asset to our choir. It was our music program that had attracted them. Some of us, like myself, were very happy to have them in the church. But there were others who were very cold to them. Finally they stopped coming, and I didn't blame them.*

The four statements just shared were all made by long-time members of a church in which Steve Clapp was doing a consultation. The primary purpose of the consultation was to help the congregation identify new strategies by which they could reach more teenagers and young adults! Those statements reveal some of the reasons why teenagers and young adults may not be overly attracted to this congregation or choose not to stay long if they do start coming.

Many churches would be delighted to have children running down the aisle for the children's story, but this congregation had several older members who were openly critical about children not being more "respectful" in worship. That is an attitude that some young parents in the congregation had clearly identified, and it was hurtful to them. These young parents felt that it was a good thing for children to be so enthused about their part of the worship service that they would run down the aisle.

The members of the youth group thought most adults in the church viewed them as alien beings, creatures from another planet or another dimension. They felt the disapproval of many in the congregation concerning their appearance. They loved the church; but like young people of every generation, they wanted to feel free to make their own choices about personal appearance and did not think of themselves as being in any way disrespectful.

The reality is that increasing numbers of young adults choose to live with each other, sometimes for extended periods of time, before they get married. And sometimes they live with each other and then make the choice not to get married. Recent figures show that children who are born "out of wedlock" are increasingly likely to be born to people in the young adult years rather than in the teenage years [U.S. Census data]. In a Christian Community study, 87% of participating young adults (ages 19–35) felt that premarital intercourse is "all right," in contrast to only 24% of older church-active adults who felt that way.

The Pew Research Center asked this question of adults: "When an unmarried man and woman have a child together, how important is it to you that they legally marry?" Among adults 65 years of age and older, 62% felt it was "very important" in contrast to 31% of those 18 to 29 years of age.

The fact that so many older adults disapprove of these trends causes hospitality problems for some congregations. It's difficult for older adults to withhold their disapproval of a living situation that they consider immoral. Yet most young adults do not see the relationship that way and resent the implication that they are doing something wrong. That leaves the young adults who are living together but unmarried with three choices: they can come to church and try to ignore the disapproval of older adults in the congregation; they can lie about their living arrangement; or they can choose not to come to church at all.

And the issue of homosexuality is a source of debate within many denominations and many congregations. The congregation discussed at the start of this chapter was fortunate to have the young gay couple attracted to it because of their music program, and one of them was clearly an asset to that program. The inability of many in the congregation to accept them, however, kept them from staying. Congregations around the country are working to rethink their attitudes toward homosexuality, and many are developing a more accepting and loving attitude toward those of a different sexual orientation.

The church in which Steve was doing the consultation was more fortunate than many because it had some children, teens, and young adults who were involved. But the intolerance and lack of hospitality of many in the congregation kept them from being able to reach more people in those age ranges and also was increasingly causing them to lose members they already had.

A church that wants to practice deep and wide hospitality toward children, youth, and young adults must have an attitude of warmth and acceptance throughout the congregation. While there are a few churches that naturally have that kind of attitude, most need to initiate educational programs to help people improve their hospitality.

Evangelism and Hospitality Training

Some people are spiritually gifted in the areas of evangelism and of hospitality. They feel comfortable talking about their faith with others, and they enjoy inviting others to worship and other church events. They take the initiative in reaching out to visitors and anyone else they don't know at church and have a natural way of helping others feel welcome and included. Many of these persons tend not to be judgmental and can show acceptance to people who may be very different from themselves.

But not every church member comes equipped with those gifts. In fact, those who work with various systems of assessing spiritual gifts tend to estimate that no more than 10% of the members of the typical church have the gift of evangelism or the gift of hospitality. And even some with the gifts of evangelism and hospitality may at times have judgmental attitudes like those shown in the church discussed at the beginning of this chapter. Christian Community's ongoing research continues to show that there are big differences in what happens on growth and assimilation between those congregations that offer instruction in evangelism and hospitality and those that do not.

Wanting to better understand what is happening in Christian education and evangelism in Protestant churches, Christian Community did a 2006 survey of leaders in 736 congregations, seeking information on their experiences in Christian education, hospitality, and outreach. The overall survey results are in the book *Hospitality and Outreach in Christian Education: Practical Strategies for Sunday Schools, Small Groups, and Other Settings.*

The following chart shows that fewer than 10% of the surveyed congregations provide training in outreach to the teachers of classes or to the classes themselves. Thirty percent of the churches provide training in outreach to some other groups in the church, but the Christian education program is clearly not a focus for that instruction.

A similar question was asked concerning training in hospitality, and that chart also follows. Hospitality refers to the warmth of the welcome that is given to new people and to the way in which people are integrated into the overall life of the congregation. The percentages of congregations providing training in hospitality to teachers and classes were even lower than those providing training in outreach. Only 21% of congregations provide training in hospitality to other groups in the church.

The failure to provide this training may be carrying a high price tag for our congregations. Christian Community research consistently shows that the majority of people in our con-

149

gregations are not comfortable with outreach (telling others about our faith in Christ and inviting people to church). More people tend to think that they know how to give a warm welcome to visitors and how to practice hospitality, but our studies show that most of our congregations are simply not as friendly as we think they are. Congregations that are growing consistently show larger percentages of members who are comfortable sharing their faith and reflect a far warmer, more pervasive hospitality within the congregation.

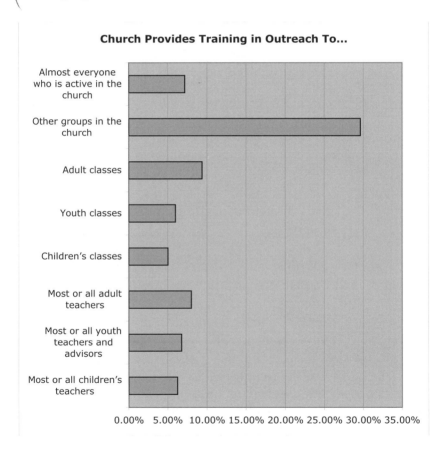

Church Provides Training in Outreach To...

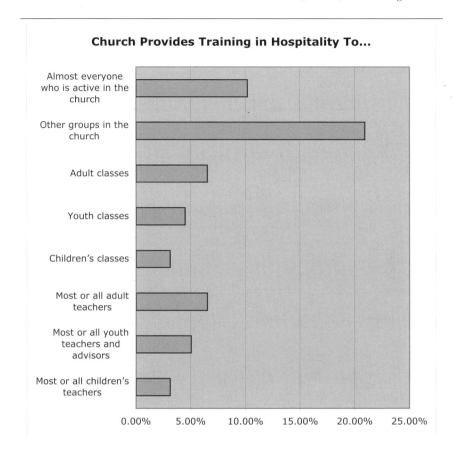

Here are some practical suggestions that can strengthen the Christian education program of a congregation and that can also result in better outreach and hospitality for the congregation as a whole.

1. If you want to have more students, add more leaders first. Having too few class or group leaders can set a growth limit on your program. The more leaders you have for a class or group, the easier it is for those persons to:

- Take the initiative in efforts to recruit new students.
- Bond quickly with new persons who come.
- Maintain class records and follow-up with guests.

151

And more! Using a team approach for classes and groups provides better leadership and also makes it easier for leaders to be gone when necessary.

2. If you want to nurture growth in the Sunday school or other classes and groups, take time periodically to talk as a group about outreach. Encourage people to bring friends to class and to social events. Children are natural evangelists and will do a great job inviting friends if encouraged to do so. Adult classes should consider studying an evangelism unit at least once a year. Adult classes can benefit from studying a book like *Sharing Living Water* by Steve Clapp and Sam Detwiler.

3. Spend time in classes talking about hospitality. Encourage people to think of those who come as guests rather than as visitors. We go out of our way to help guests feel welcomed and included. We also include guests in our social functions. Class study of books like the one you are holding and of *Widening the Welcome of Your Church* by Fred Bernhard and Steve Clapp can deepen hospitality and provide a much better understanding of how to avoid the kind of mistakes made by the church described at the beginning of this chapter.

4. Provide instruction to those who are teachers so that they in turn can provide instruction to classes. The book *Hospitality and Outreach in Christian Education* is an especially helpful resource for teachers and others working with the Christian education program of a congregation.

5. If you want to retain guests, be sure your classrooms are attractive and comfortable. Many of us become accustomed to metal chairs, rickety tables, and linoleum on the floor. What has become acceptable to us may not be attractive at all to guests who come. Attractive classrooms may not draw people to your church, but unattractive ones will surely keep them away.

6. If you want young families, be especially careful how toddler and nursery care is handled. You want these rooms to be very attractive and clean. You also want the persons in charge of care to convey confidence and security to guests. While teenagers often enjoy working in the nursery and may do a good job, be sure that you have an adult present as well.

7. If you want meaningful classes, encourage the church to recruit, train, and honor teachers. Let the Christian education program have first choice of volunteers; provide meaningful training to those who are willing to teach; and show continuing appreciation to those persons.

8. If you want to identify new children and youth, involve everyone in the church in brainstorming the names of potential guests. Take time annually to encourage the whole congregation to identify and reach out to children and youth.

9. If your church has few children and youth, don't be apologetic about broadly graded classes or about involving youth as helpers with younger classes. If your whole church appreciates children and youth, then many significant relationships will be formed. Broadly graded classes can be effective, and youth can learn by helping children learn.

Use this checklist to help determine how prepared your church is to welcome and involve guests through your Christian education program.

_____ Are teachers prepared to greet new students as they enter the classroom?

153

_____ Are teachers of children comfortable introducing themselves to the parents of guests? Do teachers know whether or not visiting children should remain in the room until their parents return?

_____ Are teachers comfortable introducing guests to the rest of the class?

_____ Do teachers provide opportunity for some sharing to help guests feel more at home?

_____ Is there a procedure to record the name, address, and phone number of any guests to a class or group?

_____ Is there a procedure for sharing information about guests with the pastor(s) and others concerned with outreach?

_____ Do adult classes have coffee and tea available?

_____ Do youth classes have juice and donuts?

_____ Are extra copies of curriculum and other study resources available for guests?

_____ Are guests informed of any coming social events and encouraged to participate?

_____ Is there a procedure for follow-up with anyone who visits a Christian education class or event?

_____ Do students in the class or group take a part in that follow-up process rather than leaving it all to the teacher or leader?

____ Are there greeters who can direct guests to the appropriate classes?

____ Are class or group members encouraged to invite friends to the group?

____ Are the classrooms all attractive, comfortable places to meet?

____ Are the rooms all neat, including updated bulletin boards?

____ Are class members encouraged to hang banners, posters, and other results of class activity?

Strategies for Greater Hospitality to Children

Most congregations want more young adult families involved. Surprisingly few, however, consider how important hospitality to children is if one wants to reach their parents. Most parents are justifiably more concerned about the meeting of the needs of their children than about the meeting of their personal needs. Here are some strategies to consider for showing greater hospitality to children in your congregation and for helping children feel assimilated into the life of the church. These strategies have much in common with those shared in the book *Widening the Welcome of Your Church*.

1. As shared in the previous section, give careful attention to the appearance, equipment, and staffing of the nursery and toddler areas.

2. Be sure that teachers and students in children's classes have received appropriate instruction in how to extend

hospitality and to reach out to persons outside the congregation. For example:

- Have leaders teach the children how to respond to guests. Like adults, children benefit from instruction in how to extend hospitality to guests. Introductions need to be made, and there should be efforts to help children learn the names of one another. Children can be taught how to show special kindness to guests.

- Students should be encouraged to reach out to their own friends who don't have church homes and invite them to Sunday school and other children's activities.

- Respond to children who are guests in a systematic way, either with a phone call or an offer to share in another activity during the week. Other children in the class can do this in the middle school and upper elementary-age classes. A teacher or the parent of a student needs to do it for younger classes.

- Leaders need to know how to respond to visiting parents—be sure they are clear on whether to pick up the children or if the children are to find them in the fellowship area (if the children are old enough to do so).

- Leaders need to follow up with those who break a pattern of regular attendance. Though many cute cards are available for this purpose ("We've been missing you" accompanied by a photo of a dog or cat, for example), a phone call usually is a better follow-up procedure. A card or letter will occasionally be misinterpreted as being critical of the absence.

- Leaders need to get the name, address, and phone number of the visitors, so that follow-up is easy to do. This information may also be useful to others working at outreach if the visitors failed to sign a guest registration for the worship service (assuming that they attended the worship service).

- Class parties are a great idea. Some classes also find it meaningful to celebrate the birthdays of students.

3. Greeters and ushers need training in how to respond to children. Children appreciate being addressed directly in conversation rather than being talked about. Adults who are especially tall sometimes bend or kneel to greet young children. Greeters should know where classrooms are for various age levels.

4. The worship service should also respond to the needs of children. Ways to accomplish that include:

- Having coloring books, crayons, or other activity materials available for children to use during the service.

- Having a "Children's Corner Cart" at the entrance to the sanctuary with books that children can read during the service.

- Having a children's choir in which children can participate.

- Having at least one part of the service which is especially focused on the needs and interests of children. This may be an anthem by the children's choir, a children's sermon, a puppet drama, or any other strategy which speaks especially to children.

- The minister and other worship leaders should model acceptance and appreciation of children. When a baby cries, a worship leader might say: "The sound of children is the sound of a healthy church!" Those who serve as greeters and ushers should be prepared to give reassurance to parents who are obviously concerned about minor behavioral problems.

- In addition to modeling acceptance and appreciation of children, the pastor should also teach the congregation why children are important to the church and how they can be helped to feel at home. Adults should place just as much priority on learning the names of children as the names of parents. No one likes to be known simply as "Fred's daughter" or "Mary's son" or "the youngest Stafford boy."

- When remodeling an existing sanctuary or building a new sanctuary, keep children in mind! Use stain-resistant carpeting and fabrics so that parents can feel free to give their children drinks in the sanctuary. Think about the comfort of the seating for children as well as for adults.

5. Junior church or children's church can be a blessing to both children and their parents. Such services make it possible for children to share in activities that are age-appropriate rather than becoming bored with the sermon and other aspects of the worship service. Some parents can participate more mean-ingfully in the worship service if they are not worrying about a fidgeting child.

Many churches choose to have children remain in the sanctuary through a children's anthem or children's sermon and then have them go to a separate location for junior church. This lets children become accustomed to the sanctuary setting and feel a part of the service without keeping them there for the entire time.

If your church is too small in membership for junior church or children's church to be realistic, don't be concerned about that. Having books to read, pictures to color, and other activities available for children can meet some of the same needs as junior church.

6. The needs of children should be taken into consideration during any kind of fellowship time. In addition to coffee and tea for adults, be sure to have cocoa or fruit drink for children. Some adults will also prefer the cocoa or fruit drink. If your church uses "silent greeters" during the fellowship time to be sure that no one is ignored, instruct those persons to be alert for the needs of children as well.

Silent greeters don't wear greeter tags and don't introduce themselves as greeters. They intentionally circulate during the fellowship time to be sure the needs of guests are being met.

Church leaders also need to model tolerance of the behavior of children during fellowship times. If children have been very quiet during worship services, they may have pent-up energy. If the fellowship area has adequate space, adults should not be upset because children choose to play games during the fellowship time.

7. Familiar faces are important to children! When class leadership is changed too quickly, new children may become disoriented and confused. Younger children especially need continuity. While many of us as adults like systems of rotating teachers and child care providers, those systems are not always the best for children who tend to like the familiarity of people they've seen before. It's also great to be present one week as a guest and to be called by name when one returns the next week.

8. Discipline problems, when they arise, need to be handled with tact and consideration. How would you want to be treated if you were a child again? How would parents want their children treated? Obviously there are not always easy answers to discipline problems, but some strategies can help:

- Having a sufficient number of adult leaders often makes a great difference. A class of fifth graders that averaged twelve out-of-control children each week became a fun, reasonably controlled fifteen when two adults leaders were added to the single teacher who had been working with the class before.

- Talking with children alone about discipline problems, if possible, is almost always preferable to doing so in front of the class.

- Appealing to children who are troublemakers to help create a better atmosphere in the class can be an effective strategy—that makes them part of the solution to the problem!

- Talking with the parents can sometimes help a class leader better understand the reasons for the behavior of children. Sometimes having the parent of a difficult child come to share in class sessions for a couple of weeks can make a difference.

9. When a church has a day care or nursery school program through the week, opportunities should be sought for the church to show hospitality to those children and their parents. This can be an excellent port of entry to the church for those with no church home. Consider:

- Having the pastor share in greeting children and their parents on at least an occasional basis.

- Having a place for information on church membership as a part of the registration process so that you can be aware of persons who do not have a church home.

- Offering occasional parties or fellowship times with refreshments for children and parents. These can be ideal opportunities for the pastor and other church leaders to visit with parents and children.

- Offering seminars on topics such as "Developing the Spiritual Life of Children" or "Creating a Secure Family Environment" to the parents of children. Have those taught by the pastor or by another church leader.

- Have low-key phone calls made, inviting parents to come with their children to worship services or to special events at the church.

- Consider having a different tuition or fee scale for persons who belong to the congregation! This rewards those who already do attend and can be a motivation for others to try out your church.

10. Be sensitive to children with special needs. Orientation for teachers should include alerting them to the fact that some children may have difficulty reading and should not be put on the spot in front of others. If students have physical, mental, or emotional limitations, some special arrangements may be appropriate. Special needs can sometimes be opportunities for innovative programs. Some congregations, for example, have begun mid-week programs for children with Attention Deficit Disorders (called, for example, ADDventure).

11. Be alert for additional program opportunities which can help meet the needs of children. Is there a need for a mid-week recreation program? A tutoring program? A Bible study group? A drama group for upper elementary children? Mid-week groups can be an especially excellent opportunity for children to bring their friends who are not part of any local church.

Some churches have started Girls' Clubs, which are mid-week opportunities for girls only. Activities include baking cookies to take to nursing homes, learning how to handle money, learning about career opportunities, painting a room in the church or a room in the home of an elderly person, going to movies together, developing a recycling program for the church, and more! A Girls' Club can meet anywhere from once a week to once a month and can be an excellent port of entry for new people into the congregation.

12. Be sure that your promotional materials and strategies make it clear that children are valued in your congregation! That should be a part of your church brochure, of any newspaper advertisements, of your church website, and of any special canvassing materials. Include pictures of children in your promotional materials.

13. Involve children who are already in your church in helping you evaluate your programs. Get their input! What would make worship and classes better? What opportunities would they like? What help do they need in extending hospitality to others?

14. Provide opportunities for children to interact with older members of the congregation. Most older persons are in fact eager for positive contact with children. Those persons who seem to be crabby toward children are often that way because they have not had sufficient opportunity to interact with children in recent years. Do things like:

- Having children give flowers to older members on a special occasion.

- Having a "secret friends" system between a children's class and an adult class.

- Having a children's class host an adult class at a dinner.

- Having a children's class survey an adult class on a particular issue.

- Having an adult class survey a children's class on a particular issue.

Strategies for Greater Hospitality to Youth

Here are some strategies to consider as you seek to show greater hospitality to youth and to help them feel more fully incorporated in the life of the congregation:

1. Remember that youth are seeking more than entertainment from the church. Young people have many places for fellowship in their lives today, and many are involved in a tremendous number of school and community activities. While the church certainly needs to offer fellowship, it is more important that the church offer prayer, Bible study, and personal growth opportunities. The church also needs to be a place where they can feel safe asking questions and being open.

Doing this kind of work with youth requires committed, mature people. There are many mature young adults who do great work with teens, but don't make the common mistake of thinking that only young adults can do youth work. Some young adults are too busy sorting out problems in their own lives to be ready for the responsibility of mentoring teens. There are churches that have had very successful youth work done by people who were in their seventies but were still young at heart. While parents are often reluctant to work with their own teens in a youth group, people the age of their parents often do excellent work with teenagers. Maturity, a genuine love of youth, and reasonable knowledge of youth culture (or at least a desire to know about youth culture) are more important requirements in youth advisors and teachers than age.

2. Welcoming congregations appreciate the fact that youth are not just the "church of tomorrow" but are in fact part of the church today. They recognize the desire of young people to make a difference in the lives of others and provide them with opportunities to do so, not only with summer mission trips but also with late afternoon, evening, or weekend service projects. They also encourage young people to be active on boards and committees of the church, often inviting them to serve in pairs for mutual support.

3. Showing hospitality to teens means accepting them as they are and not being concerned about superficial matters. Adults who work with teens and adults who interact with teens need to be helped to recognize that clothes and hair are not appropriate issues for argument in the Christian community. As uncomfortable as tattoos and tongue studs may make some adults, those should never be a basis for making teens feel unwelcome.

Teens are seeking to express their individuality and to differentiate themselves from adults. Sometimes their efforts at individuality may appear to adults simply as conformity to a different set of expectations, but we need to respect where teens are at in these decisions.

Steve Clapp recently sat with a group of adult youth advisors and teachers who were complaining about the tattoos and piercings of some of the youth in their church. Yet as the conversation progressed, it became clear that some of those in the group had themselves been criticized for long hair, torn jeans, and untied shoelaces when they were teenagers. Sometimes our memories are too short!

4. Welcoming congregations take very seriously the need to provide a "safe place" for youth. They insist that adults who work with teens and the teens themselves honor confidentiality and respect differences. Although some good-natured kidding may take place, it's important that teens not be criticized or made the victim of brutal jokes because of their differences from others in the group.

The need for confidentiality is crucial. What one teen says about sexual activity or what another teen confesses about drinking should not be spread outside the group. There may be instances when a youth leader is sufficiently concerned about the danger of suicide to feel that something must be shared with a parent, but such instances should and must be very rare—or people will not share what they really think and feel with the group.

Youth group leaders and teachers need to recognize that they may well have teens with a self-identified homosexual or bisexual orientation. Churches differ in how they view homosexuality; but whatever the doctrines of the church, it is crucial that individual teens feel accepted and feel that they are in a "safe place" in which they can explore what the Christian faith means for their lives. For more background on teens and sexuality, see the book *Faith Matters: Teenagers, Religion, and Sexuality* by Steve Clapp, Kristen Leverton Helbert, and Angela Zizak.

5. Like adults in the church, teens need to be taught how to show hospitality toward guests and to be encouraged to invite their friends to participate in church activities. You can readily modify the material in this book or in the book *Widening the Welcome of Your Church* for work with teens. *Peer Evangelism* by Steve Clapp and Sam Detwiler is another helpful resource.

6. Welcoming congregations appreciate the role food can play for youth just as it does for adults. Refreshments at youth group meetings, good food for overnight lock-ins and retreats, pizza parties to welcome new members, and meals shared between adult leaders and youth can all be part of a welcoming group atmosphere.

7. Many congregations have had considerable success with mentoring programs in which adults are paired with youth. The adult and the teenager meet together at least once a month to talk about things of concern to both of them and particularly to work on questions of values and beliefs. This approach can be especially valuable in a small congregation that doesn't have enough teens for a regular youth group or class.

Strategies for Greater Hospitality to Young Adults

Understanding the way that many young adults view the church and contemporary life can be helpful in planning ministry and outreach strategies to involve more people who are between 18 and 35 years of age. Christian Community conducted a study of the views of young adults (18–35) and older adults (36 and older) who are active in the life of 610 congregations. Young adults who are active in those churches differ significantly in their opinions on several issues in church life and in the larger society. For example:

- Young adults are much more likely to favor the legalization of marijuana.

- Young adults are much more likely to feel that sexual harassment is a major problem at their places of work.

- Young adults are somewhat more likely to feel that abortion is a decision which people have a right to make rather than always being wrong. They are also much more likely to consider it a personal moral decision and to be opposed to governmental intrusion on the right of people to prayerfully make that decision.

- Ninety-three percent of young adults feel that talking about sexual issues and concerns is a good and appropriate thing to do in church settings; only 39% of older adults agree with that view.

- Young adults are more likely to feel that there are circumstances in which divorce is "necessary" for the well-being of both partners and sometimes for the well-being of their children.

- Young adults are well over twice as likely to feel that homosexuality is an acceptable lifestyle and to feel that homosexuality is not something that people "choose" but rather that some people simply "are" homosexual.

- Eighty-seven percent of the young adults in the study feel that premarital intercourse is "all right," in contrast to only 24% of older church-active adults who feel that way.

- Young adults are more likely to feel comfortable working with computers and to spend daily time on the Internet, though there is evidence that gap is decreasing.

- Older adults are much more likely to feel that the political system in their country "works" (both in the United States and Canada). They are also more likely to feel that having a strong military is important, though older Canadians did not see that as important as older United States residents did.

- Even though they are active in the life of a congregation, 74% of the younger adults do not feel that church involvement is "essential" to the faith in contrast to 21% of older adults. Sixty-one percent of the young adults feel that the church functions too much like any other institution in society in contrast to 31% of older adults.

When one considers that such great differences exist in perspective between young adults and older adults who are active in the church, it is not surprising that it is difficult to retain young adult involvement and to reach new young adults. In that study, 87% of the young adults who are church-active said that they "withheld their beliefs and opinions a significant amount of the time because they knew older members would disapprove of their views."

Recognizing the existence of such differences, what are some of the strategies that congregations can use to improve their hospitality to young adults? We especially recommend:

1. Help older adults in the church better understand the perspective of young adults both inside and outside of the church. Your involvement of church groups in a study of this book is one way to accomplish that. When possible, involve both young adults and older adults in the study process so that you have good sharing.

2. Implement as many of the suggestions as possible for providing greater hospitality to children. Creating an atmosphere attractive to children is one of the best possible ways to create an atmosphere which is welcoming for their parents.

3. Help members of the congregation be sure that they are just as welcoming to young singles and to couples who do not have children as they are to young couples with children. Young adult couples who do not have children are often not appreciative of the suggestion that surely they'll be starting to have them soon! Even if your church doesn't have any young adult singles, it's still possible to warmly welcome singles who visit. Older members of the congregation sometimes "adopt" young adult singles, inviting them into their homes for meals and taking an interest in their lives. When you've gotten a few guests transformed to active participants, you have the core group for a young singles group. The same can be true for married couples without children.

4. Make a special effort to help older members understand the unique circumstances of single parents. Many single parents are very interested in spiritual issues and in what the church at its best can offer, but are quickly turned off by the implied disapproval of their unmarried or divorced status.

Classes and groups designed to help people become more welcoming need to point out the importance of not immediately asking someone where his or her spouse is. There may not be a spouse!

5. Encourage more open discussion of sexuality within your congregation. As shared, younger adults and older adults often do not feel the same about premarital intercourse and homosexuality. They may also not feel the same way about the nature of marriage. Many of us have not seriously considered these issues, and our churches have been reluctant to discuss such potentially controversial topics.

A full consideration of these issues goes beyond the scope of this book. We do feel, however, that it is crucial for churches to become less judgmental and more welcoming. For more guidance, see Debra Haffner's publication *A Time to Build: Creating Sexually Healthy Faith Communities*. Another approach can be to involve older and younger adults in a study of how to help teenagers with sexual decision-making utilizing the book *Faith Matters: Teenagers, Sexuality, and Religion*; that study of teens and sexuality can also provide opportunity for adults to share their own views. The booklet *Taking a New Look: Why Congregations Need LG BT Members* can help your church become more accepting of gay, lesbian, bisexual, and transgender persons.

6. Recognize the need for variety in worship services. For some congregations this means starting a contemporary service. For others it means integrating more contemporary elements such as songs and drama into an existing service. Help people understand the reasons for such changes, and continue interpreting those reasons. For more help on this, see the book *Worship and Hospitality* by Steve Clapp and Fred Bernhard and *The Alternative Worship Primer* by Cindy Hollenberg.

7. Be prepared to more quickly integrate enthusiastic young adults into the life of the church. Don't wait until annual elections to invite people to serve on a board, commission, committee, or task force in which they are interested.

8. If your church is to be sensitive to the needs of young adults on a continuing basis, then you need to have persons of that age range as members of the major decision-making groups in your congregation. That way their perspective is always available.

9. Recognize the reality that young adults who have not grown up in the church may not be familiar with many things which the rest of us take for granted. For a fuller discussion of this, see the book *Widening the Welcome of Your Church.*

10. Provide many opportunities for young adults and older adults to interact with one another. Differences in perspective are not as important when people know and like one another. Some young adults and older adults reading this book will feel that they do not have the differences in perspective that are described. Where that is the case, it is very often because healthy interactions between young adults and older adults are a regular part of the life of the congregation.

11. Consider a decision-making structure in your church that is less complicated and that incorporates greater trust. Young adults are often not as patient as older adults with the slow decision-making process that dominates many congregations. Sharing specific models for church organization goes beyond the scope of this book, but it is crucial to recognize that truly welcoming young adults generally means moving toward a less restrictive and more permission-giving church organization. There are large numbers of older adults in most congregations who would also like to see some changes in this direction.

The main barrier to streamlining church organizational structures and decision-making processes is that it requires a greater degree of trust. People must be willing to trust others to make decisions and to be supportive of groups with which they are not personally involved. Large congregations are more likely to have such an atmosphere because of the impossibility of a significant percentage of the membership being involved in every decision. Smaller congregations which have functioned for years with systems that required broad agreement before any change was made may find it initially difficult to let decisions be made more rapidly and by fewer people. Failure to make that transition, however, can have a very limiting effect on church growth.

Growing churches are increasingly characterized by:

- A structure that emphasizes DOING more than DECIDING. There are fewer decision-making groups and more action groups.

- A structure with fewer standing committees and more task forces or mission groups appointed as needs arise.

- A greater willingness to trust individuals and groups to make decisions without having several layers of approval.

- A clearer separation of those decisions having significant impact on the whole congregation and needing the involvement of many persons from those decisions which affect only a few people or are of relatively minor importance.

And if you come upon the perfect organizational structure for your church, which suits persons of all ages, PLEASE send the details of the structure to the authors of this book! We'd love to have it. For the present, most of us are in transition, seeking to make improvements at the pace that our congregations can accept.

As Chapter Six has shown, there are significant gaps between the way that many older adults and many younger adults view premarital intercourse, homosexuality, and a number of other issues. Persons who are convinced that such behaviors are immoral, of course, cannot grant approval to persons practicing those acts. A harsh and judgmental attitude toward younger adults on these matters, however, is guaranteed to stop any chance of dialogue and is likely to keep young adults away from the community of faith. Many older adults have young adult children who have had premarital intercourse and who have chosen to live with each other before marriage. An increasing number of persons have family members who have come out as gay or lesbian. We are living in a time when dialogue on these matters has become very important. Many people are studying the issues and looking again to see what Scripture does and does not say on these matters.

Chapter Seven
Entry Points and Deeper Relationships

Acts 2:42–47

Concept: There are many different entry points into the life of a congregation, and all of them are important. Regardless of the initial point of entry and the initial experiences in the church, people will only continue to come if they have been helped to develop and maintain deeper relationships with God and with one another. Even long-time members can have experiences that alienate them from the congregation.

The Hunger for Acceptance

Janice was a junior in college when she became pregnant. She regretted having had sex with the young man and thought woefully about the reality that they had not even gone out with each other for three weeks. She also regretted not having used contraception, both of them having failed to anticipate that their arousal would take them so far so fast.

She had grown up in a congregation that had a strong pro-life stance, and she remembered what she had been taught there. She made several important decisions:

- She was not going to marry the father of the child. It had been a mistake to go out with him and to have sex with him. She didn't love him, and he didn't love her. There was no point in compounding bad decisions by adding the bad decision of marriage.

- She was not going to have an abortion. It was against what she had been taught at church, and it was against her own moral code. If she had been raped or the baby were likely to be born with significant disabilities, she might have considered it. But all that was involved here was the carelessness of two people, and she was not about to have an abortion under these circumstances.

- She knew that she would need a lot of help emotionally and spiritually to get through the pregnancy and the first months with the child. She decided to return to her hometown and live with her parents until after the child was born. She felt sure she could count on the support of her parents and of her home congregation.

Janice's parents embraced her and were thankful that she wanted to come home and let them help her through the months ahead. She did not want to have the baby adopted, and they worked with her to determine a strategy for her to have the baby, enroll in a college closer to their home, and receive the child care help she needed from them.

When her current semester ended, Janice came home. She knew it was the right decision, and she was immensely thankful for the acceptance and help of her parents. She started attending her home congregation right away, and she was open with people about the reason for her decision to come home.

People in the church initially welcomed her. She was invited to join a young adult social group right away. The others in the group were married, but she was encouraged to participate. She was also invited to help teach a kindergarten Sunday school class, and she began looking forward to that each week.

When the reality that she was pregnant became obvious in her physical appearance, Janice started to notice a shift in the way people in the church were relating to her. She would approach a group of people during fellowship time on Sunday morning and get the feeling that they immediately changed the topic of their conversation as she walked up to them. She felt that the greetings from some members were just a little cooler than they had been before.

Then she was approached by the Sunday school superintendent who suggested to her that it might be better for her not to continue helping teach the kindergarten class since she was so obviously pregnant. He thought some of the parents were a little uneasy about a single, pregnant person being in a position of trust and responsibility. He named two couples who were in the young adult group, and that made her feel uncomfortable continuing to participate in those social activities.

An elderly, influential member of the congregation approached Janice and shared with her the concern "some people" had that her presence wasn't sending a good message to the teenagers in the congregation. The church didn't want to take a chance that their appearing to accept her unmarried pregnancy would cause some-one else in the congregation to have sex before marriage.

Janice got the message. She quit coming to church. The first couple of Sundays she missed, the minister contacted her by phone to see if she was all right. Janice claimed morning sickness both times rather than tell him what others had said to her.

When she had missed four consecutive Sundays, her minister came to her home to talk with her. In a tearful conversation, Janice told him what had happened. He apologized to her on behalf of the church and encouraged her to start coming again, but she refused. She said that she was not going to go where she clearly was not welcome.

The minister attended a meeting of the church's Board of Elders and told them what had happened. "This," he said, "is the first time that I have been ashamed of our church. Janice chose not to have an abortion in large part because of what she had been taught in this congregation. She came back here to have the child feeling that she would find love and support. Instead, she's found a judgmental attitude at the very point in time when she most needed love. She's made it very clear the pregnancy was a mistake. I absolutely cannot believe that her presence will send any wrong message to a teenager in this church. If it does, then shame on us for not having done a better job teaching them our values. We need to fix this."

Four members of the Board of Elders went to Janice's home to visit with her. They were apologetic, and they also made clear to Janice that they felt the church needed for her to return so that they could become a more accepting, better congregation. Janice was moved by their sincerity and came back to church the following Sunday.

This was a congregation that did not practice infant baptism but did have a service of dedication for infants and young children. On the Sunday that Janice presented her baby for dedication, she and her parents went to the front of the sanctuary at the appropriate time in the worship service. The minister came to the point in the liturgy where he asked for those who would be godparents to this child to stand. Godparents, in that church's tradition, were people who would offer emotional, spiritual, and, if needed, even financial support to the child and parent(s). One couple in the church had been chosen by Janice for that purpose.

When the minister asked the godparents to stand, they did so. Then almost immediately every member of the Board of Elders stood. And then the entire congregation stood in a unanimous show of support of Janice and her child.

The minister who shared this account with Steve Clapp made this observation: "I went from being ashamed of the congregation for the first time to being absolutely proud, in a healthy way, of their response. The woman who had earlier told Janice not to come to church was one of the first people to stand. This experience really changed us as a congregation. We learned what it means to truly be accepting of others. And we also learned how damaging our judgmentalism can be. The Holy Spirit has really been working in our church through this experience. Janice and her baby have been a great blessing to us."

People do hunger for acceptance. That's true for guests who have come for the first time. That's true for prospective members. That's true for new members. And that's true for people who have been in the church for a very long period of time.

Janice had literally grown up in that church. She returned to it during a time of enormous personal need. Some people return to church or come to church for the first time because they are facing a spiritual, emotional, physical, or financial crisis in their lives that pulls them toward God and the community of faith. Some people return to church or come for the first time because of the encouragement of a friend, neighbor, family member, or coworker.

People may start coming to worship, to a Sunday school class, to the choir, to a service project, to a social event, or to some other church activity. Whatever the entry point, they will continue coming only if they feel that their church experiences are bringing them closer to God and to one another. Even people who have been in the church for years can have experiences that make them feel shut out or unaccepted.

The failure to feel accepted and to feel wrapped in caring relationships isn't always as dramatic as that of Janice and may in fact be easier to miss. Brad and Mary moved into a new community and had been attending First Church for three months. They had initially planned to "shop around" for a congregation, but the warm welcome at First Church made them decide to stay.

The solid initial hospitality of the church was reflected in many ways. The nametags had a special designation for guests. And so greeters, ushers, and other congregational members took special care to surround them with warm welcomes. The worship service was well planned, the music uplifting, and the message by the senior pastor was biblically based and inspiring.

At the end of the service the pastor reminded everyone of the refreshment time in the fellowship hall following the service, and invited guests who were present to join them. There are congregations in which guests are overlooked by long-time members who are eager to connect with each other, but that wasn't the case at First Church. Mary and Brad found people taking the initiative to greet them, and they even received invitations to go out to lunch.

After three months, however, the church didn't feel quite the same to Mary and Brad. People they had met still called them by name, but it was clear that the social networks of the church were not open. There were no more invitations to lunch, even though it was clear that many others were getting together after worship.

Brad and Mary had received a couple of invitations to evening events at the church, but it hadn't been possible to come because of their busy schedule. Word spread in the congregation that this new couple probably didn't want to be involved, so the invitations stopped. The two of them had been sincere in saying they had prior commitments those evenings, but members inaccurately concluded they were not interested.

They tried a Sunday school class, but discovered that this class of couples their age had a "history." The small talk preceding the study of the day always left them out. They couldn't relive or identify with that extremely humorous prank that the men played on the women five years before at the class retreat. No one ever told them what was so funny. Learning to know relational connections in the class was a challenge. At times the illustrations used in the lesson brought up some event that was only known by long-time class members. So here were Brad and Mary, a new couple in what many considered to be the friendliest church in town, but unable to form any friendships.

Building Relationships in Groups

Every church that reaches new people faces the challenge of seeing that they are not lost following the initial weeks and months of involvement. They need to form meaningful relationships with people in the congregation and to become part of the social networks of the church.

People do not form close friendships with hundreds of people. In fact, people generally do not form close relationships in a church with more than sixty or so people. If a church has only fifty or sixty members, then meaningful relationships may indeed be formed with everyone in the faith community. In most churches, however, the number of close friendships a person, couple, or family has will not extend to the entire congregation, though people may know a large number of people by name after several months of involvement. While knowing people by name is valuable, it isn't the same as having a meaningful friendship.

People need to find meaningful points of connection with others and also find settings in addition to worship that help them in their development of deeper connections with God. The church doesn't want people like Brad and Mary to be lost after the initial weeks and months as guests. The church also doesn't want people ike Janice to have hurtful experiences that cause them to disappear from the life of the church. There are a number of strategies that can be used to help keep these problems from occurring or to identify and correct them quickly when they do. For example:

1. As shared in Chapter Four, a system of faith friends or partners can help nurture a full assimilation of new people. A faith friend can take many initiatives to see that new people become well connected with longer-time members. Likewise a faith friend can notice and respond when someone who has been regular in involvement breaks that pattern of attendance. If Brad and Mary had been assigned faith friends, there would have been more consistent initiatives to get them connected.

2. Congregations often find that a formal system of deacons, shepherds, caregivers, or neighborhood coordinators can help see that the needs of people are met and that people receive the help they need to deal with difficult situations. Congregations often divide the membership into deacon or shepherd or neighborhood groups with a person or couple assigned to provide support and encouragement to the people in a particular group. Some churches with a long heritage of deacons looking out for the needs of the membership have continued that designation. An increasing number of churches are using the terminology of shepherds, caregivers, or neighborhood coordinators.

People can be assigned to groups on the basis of where they live, in which case the neighborhood coordinator terminology works well. In other instances, however, especially in very urban areas, geographical areas may not be meaningful. It may be better to make assignments on the basis of common interests, length of time as members (with an effort to have both newer and long-time members in each group), or some other system.

Generally speaking the deacon, shepherd, caregiver, or neighborhood coordinator will not be assigned more than eight to twelve households. The specific responsibilities of persons assigned these groups may vary considerably, but this list shares how some churches have defined the role:

Caregiver Responsibilities

- Try to be aware of the attendance patterns of the people for whom you are the caregiver. If someone breaks a regular pattern of attendance, follow up to see if they are having a problem or a need to which the church should respond. The church office will notify you when someone who has been regular in attendance is absent for six consecutive weeks, but you can feel free to respond whenever you become aware of an absence of three weeks or longer. A phone call is generally the best way to respond.

- Some caregivers send birthday cards and anniversary cards to the people assigned to them. The church office will provide you with a list of birthdays and anniversaries. [We don't provide the year of birth because some people like to keep that confidential!]

- When the church has a special emphasis, the office will contact you and ask you to call those on your caregiving list to encourage their involvement.

- If you have people on your list who are shut-ins or who have significant health problems, contact them at an interval that feels comfortable to you to see if there is anything that can be done to help them. You may at times decide to involve others in the helping process, especially if someone needs help with transportation or meals for an extended period of time.

- When someone new is assigned to your caregiving group, call or visit that person to introduce yourself and to let that person know the church is ready to help should they have any needs. Sometimes people who have recently moved into the community and started attending our church will appreciate help getting to know the community and community services.

- Be alert for opportunities to reach out to people who do not have a church home. If someone new moves into your neighborhood, introduce yourself to that person, find out if he or she has a church home, and extend an invitation to our congregation if appropriate!

- Some caregivers have a social event in their home once or twice a year and invite all those on their caregiving list to take part. This might be a potluck meal, a summer cookout, coffee and dessert, or a Christmas gathering (without gifts!). If you don't feel comfortable doing this in your home, feel free to ask someone on your list to host the event or to have it at the church.

The preceding description clearly has some potential overlap with a faith friends program for new people. Usually people are not assigned to a caregiving group until they have been attending for several weeks and appear likely to join. The main responsibility for keeping new people involved should remain with the faith friend, but assignment to a caregiving group sends a message of belonging and acceptance to the guest or potential member.

There can be reasons for a new person being assigned to a caregiver besides that person being new to the church. The change in assignment might come about because of a geographical move on the part of that person or because of an effort to better balance the caregiver lists.

As shared before, assignments to deacons, shepherds, or caregivers are not always done on the basis of geography. And being alert for potential members is obviously something that everyone in the congregation should be encouraged to do. People in the deacon, shepherd, caregiver, or neighborhood coordinator role, however, are especially likely to be alert for new people who move into their neighborhood, even if their assigned persons are not concentrated geographically.

3. Maintain regular attendance records, especially at worship and in Christian education settings; and have a clear plan for response when people break a pattern of regular attendance. As shared earlier in this book, when the church follows up within six weeks of a break in regular attendance, the probability of that person returning to involvement is 95%. When the church delays six months or longer from the start of the break in attendance, then the probability of that person returning drops to 25%.

If a church has a deacon, shepherd, caregiver, or neighborhood coordinator system in place, those persons are the best ones to follow up on breaks in attendance, particularly from worship services. If your church does not have such a system, then a pastor or a volunteer can do the follow-up. Breaks in attendance patterns from Sunday school, small groups, choirs, prayer groups, and other such settings are generally best handled by a member of the group.

The maintenance of records on worship attendance needs to be done for the congregation as a whole with some kind of system of attendance recording on Sunday morning. Some very small churches simply have a volunteer who maintains an attendance record each week. Most churches, however, find that they need some kind of attendance registration system. One of the most useful systems is that of having a pad provided in the pew which everyone signs and which can then be passed back down the row, letting others know who is in the pew.

While it is good for people like deacons, shepherds, caregivers, or neighborhood coordinators to pay attention to whether or not people assigned to them are present at worship, this is not a reliable strategy in any but the smallest of congregations. A more formal system of attendance records is important in most con-gregations. Many churches have computer software that makes it easy to enter attendance records and to print reports on persons who have been present or absent.

Also as shared earlier in this book, a phone call is the best initial follow-up on a break in attendance. Notes and e-mail can be misunderstood, and a visit to the home may be an overreaction. A phone call makes it possible to convey the message that the person was missed and to discover if there is a problem. If a person who has been contacted by phone continues to miss, then a visit to the home becomes appropriate and needed.

4. The existing small group structure of the church can be utilized to be sure people have good face-to-face connections with others. Congregations have a wide range of settings that bring people into closer connection:

- Sunday school classes
- Midweek Christian education classes
- Prayer groups
- Bible study groups
- Choirs and other musical groups
- Commissions, committees, task forces, and mission groups
- Service groups
- Small groups
- Social groups
- Athletic groups
- Quilting groups

And so the list could be continued!

Prospective members and new members should be invited to participate in groups appropriate to their interests. While many of these groups have a stated purpose like education, Bible study, music, or coordinating activities, involvement in the groups also helps people in building relationships. Groups should be encouraged to be sensitive to the needs of those who participate and also to follow-up when someone who has been involved breaks that pattern of involvement.

A growing number of congregations are doing more with the concept of **mission groups**. Mission groups are usually organized for a specific purpose, often a ministry of service. Mission groups can be organized to run a food pantry, to run a children's program, to paint houses for the poor, to work for improved education in the community, to raise funds for a mission in another country, to work for HIV/AIDS prevention in the community, or for many other purposes. These groups are often open to anyone who wishes to participate with no nomination, election, or term limitation process. They are often great places for involvement of new people who can immediately begin participating. Young adults are especially likely to prefer these groups that have a focus on doing rather than on decision-making.

5. A growing number of congregations have moved to a formal small group process that intentionally involves everyone in the congregation (who is willing) in a small group. This is an especially common strategy in new church starts that from the very beginning have everyone assigned to a small group. An intentional effort is generally made to mix longer-time members and new members in the small groups.

The twelve disciples of Christ were an effective small group! While the disciples came from very different walks of life, including fishermen and a tax collector, they were united by our Lord. It was in the intimate presence of Christ that they found the strength to remain solid in their faith. Their bonds with each other and with their Lord provided the foundation for the spread of the Christian faith and the church.

The spread of early Methodism was initiated when John and Charles Wesley drew great crowds of people through their mass meetings. That was the entry point. But the genius of the movement was through a method of nurturing and instructing new Christians through what were called *class meetings*. People were brought together in small groups for mutual encouragement, for prayer, for Bible study, and for equipping as disciples. The *methodical* nature of the movement was responsible for the name Methodist.

During the 1980s the Meserete Kristos Church in Ethiopia, Africa, composed of 7,000 members, went underground when the Communists took over. Many leaders were captured and imprisoned. The church surreptitiously divided up into small groups of twelve to fifteen people. These groups continued to multiply as new people were invited to study the Bible, pray, and worship. In eight years the membership in this church grew in small groups from 7,000 to about 50,000! There is power in the fellowship, support, and worship of small groups.

Remember that it takes more effort to integrate new people into long-established classes and groups. Many rapidly growing churches work on the principle of "new groups for new people" and are quick to form new class and group opportunities. Healthy assimilation in a church really means both forming new groups and teaching people in existing groups how to better integrate new people.

There are many different approaches to forming an overall small group program for a congregation, and over a hundred books have been written about those approaches. Ed Bontrager spent time studying the small group approach of Cape Christian Fellowship in Florida, which modeled their work on that of Northpoint Community Church in Atlanta, Georgia. The next section describes that strategy.

"Foyer—Living Room—Kitchen Table"

The image of the church as family is a common and powerful one, though it has limitations. A congregation of several hundred or thousand people is a very large family, and it is not realistic to think that everyone will know everyone. Even the largest congregation, however, can provide smaller groupings and opportunities for people to develop close, caring relationships. The Cape Christian/Northpoint model uses the symbolism of a family's home to describe the process of assimilation. The "kitchen table" represents the ultimate expression of fellowship and life in the family.

When new people first begin attending a function at the church, they are known as being in the "foyer" stage—they are just meeting the family. They shake hands with people, exchange names with some, and start to get just a little feel for the congregation. For most people, the foyer stage means attendance at an initial worship service or two. Some people don't begin their contact with the church through worship but do so through a Sunday school class, a social event, or another opportunity.

The "living room" stage is a good second step. The persons in the "living room" begin to get involved but have not really developed any close friendships. They do a little visiting and exchanging of ideas, but the conversations are not deep ones.

Sitting in the living room is the natural progression when someone new comes to visit one's home. We wouldn't think of leaving guests standing in the foyer for thirty minutes. So settling

the couch for a while provides an opportunity to catch up
on the weather, tell each other about recent trips you each have
taken, talk a bit about your children, and discuss the latest local or
worldwide news story (if the topic feels reasonably safe!). The
relationship is slowly beginning to build, but there's no guarantee
yet that people will come again.

The "living room" for the church guests in many congregations
may take the form of:

- Going out to brunch with a church member or members
  who have invited them.

- Having a visit in their own home with a volunteer from the
  church or with a staff member. Usually the first time a
  person from the church comes by the home of the guest the
  conversation is just one at the door as the church volunteer
  leaves a small gift and shares appreciation for the guest
  having been present. The "living room" stage is a more
  substantial one and is generally the result of an
  appointment having been made.

- Having a visit in the home of a person from the church who
  has invited them to come for a meal or for dessert.

Some congregations that have a good flow of visitors have a
carry-in meal for guests at the church. This can be another "living
room" event. It is an excellent way for guests and church leadership to become acquainted, as each shares briefly his or her story,
and the pastor has an opportunity to provide some basic orientation. This may lead to a decision by guests to attend a formal
membership class or orientation session. Getting people interested
in formal membership, however, is not the primary goal.

The goal is to get people to the "kitchen table" where they are moved to a deeper level of involvement with Christ and with others in the Christian community. In many congregations, this means getting them involved in a small group that has the purpose of nurturing the faith and of nurturing relationships.

At Cape Christian Fellowship, the "kitchen table" takes the form of what they call "Life Groups." That's where the action is. Their Life Groups are composed of eight to twelve people, and those groups have been one of the most important factors in the congregation growing from three church-planting couples twenty years ago to an attendance of 1,200 each Sunday morning. Life Groups have helped hundreds of people of all ages and from all backgrounds become assimilated into Cape Christian Fellowship, and enfolded into God's family.

There are seven "checkpoints" for the Life Groups at Cape Christian Fellowship. These checkpoints embody the philosophy and the organizational structure of these small groups:

1. Personal Growth: People in the groups are committed to deepening their relationships with Christ.

2. Share Ownership: Group members share responsibility for the group. Group members help with food, follow-up, and the curriculum. While there is a designated leader for each group, the group itself chooses an assistant leader.

3. Meet Regularly: Life Groups meet at least two times a month.

4. Open Door: People are invited to join a new group at the beginning of each series. Group participants are encouraged to invite new people to participate.

5. Meeting: The leaders of the groups get together at least twice a year, once for a party and once for training.

6. Consultation: Each Life Group leader will have a coach to consult on all matters of group dynamics and development.

7. Leadership Training: There is training for the leaders of these groups and a curriculum to help study and discussion.

Even though one of the seven checkpoints is to invite new people, bringing new people into the groups isn't always easy. Some people feel such a strong sense of belonging in a group that they find it difficult to accept new people. There is a benefit in encouraging some change in the groups when a new series is begun. An assistant leader and three or four others can split off to form a new group, thus creating some openings in the existing group.

Growing congregations often make it clear to people when groups are formed that adding new people is a major purpose of the groups. Thus a time will come when some people leave the group to form a new one and to create openings in the existing group as well. This gives more people the opportunity for relationship building and spiritual growth. From time to time the group is reminded of this goal, so that when that time of group division comes in order to add new people, group members are expecting it. There are no surprises. The separation may still be difficult, but the pain is reduced because group members see a larger goal.

Historians tell us that in the first few centuries there was a rigid orientation into Christianity. Often it took a whole year of catechetical classes before baptism was administered. People in these Greek and Roman cultures were coming out of rank paganism. If we wish to assimilate those who have little or no

Christian background, our discipleship programs must extend over months and years. Integrating these persons into Life Groups or cell groups of some type will be the long-term solution for keeping people connected and helping them to continue growing in the faith.

Some churches take the strategy of placing prospective members and new members into groups with others who are new to the church. Certainly it can be easier to bring new people together than to integrate them with long-time members. Not integrating long-time members and new members, however, can leave significant gaps in the assimilation process and also can deprive people of the benefits of coming together.

The integrating of long-time members with new members has the distinct advantage of older members hearing what it's like for a new person to fit into the church. Sometimes the new member has concerns or suggestions that long-time members need to hear. It's also good for new people to learn about the faith struggles of long-time members and also to learn about the church's history.

A Primer for Starting Small Groups

Starting and promoting a small group ministry can be extremely valuable not only in assimilating new people but in nurturing the spiritual and relationship growth of everyone in the congregation. Here's one set of guidelines on how to start a small group ministry.

1. To begin small groups there must be a few people, along with the pastor, who have a vision for this ministry. It is clear that this ministry cannot be detached from the structure of the church, since there needs to be some accountability to the larger body. Since it is a ministry organized and sponsored by the church, there

should be public knowledge that a small group ministry is beginning, so that it does not become viewed as a secret operation.

2. Those interested in forming such a group should develop a list of persons to invite. They should also determine the topic or purpose for the group, the number of weeks it will meet, and day and time for meetings. Then that information can be shared with those being invited to participate. The topic or purpose of the group can be varied and might include:

- Being a prayer group for the church and the world.
- Being a spiritual growth group for all participants.
- Being a Bible study group.
- Being a group that identifies a social problem and works together to improve life for others.

A Bible study resource or a small group curriculum can be especially helpful in the first several weeks that a group meets.

3. A small group should begin with seven to eight people. That leaves room for three or four new people to be invited to participate after meetings have begun. The group should ideally have both a leader and an assistant leader. Then if there is a decision to divide the group after a certain amount of time, there will be a leader for both the new group and the continuing group.

4. At the end of the ten to twelve sessions, the group could consider dividing—in order to multiply the number of participants. One plan would be for seven or eight to remain with the original leader and then for four or five new members to be added. Sometimes groups decide to divide into two new groups of equal size. Groups larger than twelve are generally too big for the kind of highly personal sharing that one hopes will be a part of the small group experience.

5. Individual participants or someone taking notes for the group as a whole should keep track of prayer requests, decisions made, progress made, and any other information that it would be valuable to review the following week.

6. If a group divides to form two groups, it can sometimes be valuable for the two groups to come together for a social event.

7. Members of a small group should be asked to make a pledge or commitment to such things as:
- I will pray daily for each person in my group.
- I will come to every group meeting unless I am sick or faced with an unusual job or family need.
- I will keep confidential the things that are shared within the small group.

8. The small group should be a setting in which people can feel free to acknowledge their social, emotional, spiritual, physical, or even financial needs. There are few places in our society where people feel comfortable doing this. The small group should be such a place.

9. Many small groups find it beneficial to begin by having each person talk about his or her spiritual journey. What were their earliest experiences of God? How has their relationship with Jesus Christ affected their lives? What have been spiritual highs and lows that they have experienced?

10. The gifts and talents of people should be utilized in the small group when appropriate. This can include gifts of prayer, music, organization, and Bible study. The small group experience often results in people having a far better understanding of the gifts and talents of others in the group. The spiritual gifts process shared in Chapter Five can be a valuable activity for a new small group.

A church focused on outreach will see small groups as foundation stones for assimilation and growth. However, members in the maintenance-oriented church sometimes see groups as cliques or closed clubs. Even leadership can see them as threatening to other programs of the church. For example, it is not difficult to surmise that members would become perplexed and even disturbed if ten or twelve people decide to meet in a home setting on Wednesday evening instead of attending a mid-week service or prayer meeting at church. Church leaders focused on mission, in contrast, will rejoice to see this multiplication of groups, especially if new people are building relationships and growing in their faith in these more informal settings.

Other Entry Points

As shared at the end of Chapter Four, there need to be at least seven small groups or units in the church for every 100 members. Also, one out of six groups should have started in the last two years.

Though many growing churches around the world have ascertained that having small groups is an excellent means for incorporating and keeping members, congregations have discovered other ways to help assimilate members. Existing groups within the congregation can be good entry points for new people and can help in the assimilation process. Think carefully about the number of group opportunities within your congregation.

1. Sunday School Classes and Other Ongoing Christian Education Groups. When most of the people in an existing Sunday school class have been together for a long time and have developed a good knowledge of the Bible and of the faith, they may not always be comfortable settings for new members. People who transfer from other churches can often be integrated into a

Sunday school class if their biblical knowledge is about the same as that of others in the group. It also helps, of course, if someone in the class has been a long-time friend of a new person in the church. People who have not had previous involvement in the life of a congregation, however, may find it more difficult to be integrated into an existing Sunday school class.

There are two ways of dealing with this situation. First, it is possible to improve the hospitality in any Sunday school class. The fact that people are at different points in their knowledge of the Bible and in their faith journeys does not have to be a barrier to enjoying learning and sharing together. Here are things that can help in this process:

- Have existing classes study the book you are holding in your hands right now or Fred Bernhard and Steve Clapp's book *Widening the Welcome of Your Church*. That kind of study can increase the awareness of class members of the need for hospitality that goes beyond a handshake and improve sensitivity to the needs of visitors and new members.

- Keep attendance records for the class, and pay attention to any break in attendance pattern. Reach out with a phone call anytime someone who has been regular in attendance stops coming, whether that person is a new member or someone who has been coming for many years. Remember that when contact is made relatively early after a break in attendance, the probability that the person will return to regular activity is about 95%.

- Work to keep the social networks of the class open to new people. Members of most long-time Sunday school classes have extensive friendship networks in the class that go beyond study on Sunday morning. Be sure that lunch and supper invitations get extended to newer people.

Second, many congregations can benefit by forming new adult Sunday school classes or other Christian education groups. The formation of a new class or group provides opportunity for everyone to start on an equal footing.

2. Fellowship Activities. Eating together at Sunday noon carry-in meals, home meals, special banquets, and dining out provide venues that help bring people together. Fortunately, many churches are becoming more multicultural. Therefore, our fellowship events and food choices can reflect that. Some denominations love to schedule potlucks—when every family brings their favorite dish to share. These can be especially great events as a congregation becomes more multicultural and that is reflected in the dishes that are shared.

Times of fellowship can potentially be lonely for prospective members and new members, especially if they have not yet joined an existing class or group or lack a friendship partner or faith friend. Long-time members are sometimes too quick to look for a table with people who have been friends for many years—rather than intentionally seeking out people they do not know as well. Those planning fellowship events should make arrangements to be sure that newer people are joined by long-time people.

And if a congregation develops a true spirit of deep and wide hospitality, all those who are participating will be motivated to reach out to those they do not know as well. While it's good to have specific persons who make it a point to be sure new people do not sit by themselves, it's even better to have a pervasive hospitality in the congregation.

3. Service Projects. Working together results in emotional and social bonding. Projects at home or abroad bring servant-hearted people together to contribute to the good of society. New members, long-time members, and many people outside the church have an inward drive to make a better world. If this is so, what better way to assimilate new people within the fellowship than to invite them to use their skills to:

- Help clean up after a hurricane in a distant state?
- Help build a Habitat for Humanity house in your local area?
- Start a soup kitchen in the church?
- Start an after-school children's ministry?
- Form a Girls' Club for girls in the church and in the community?
- Form an Adventure Group for boys in the church and in the community?
- Start a new youth group?
- Join an overseas mission team serving in an impoverished country?
- Develop strategies to improve public school education in the community?
- Develop a ministry to persons with HIV/AIDS?
- Do a recycling education program for the community?

Working together, planning together, and traveling together can forge deep bonds with people of varying backgrounds. Groups focusing on such needs can effectively bring together long-time members, new members, prospective members, and even people outside of the church. We often forget that the motivation to help others runs deep within many people who have been disappointed in the institutional church. Opportunities to share in service can be very attractive to some of these people.

4. Other Church Settings. As shared before, remember that there are many different entry points into the life of the church; and all of those entry points offer opportunities to help assimilate people and nurture people. Does your church have:

- Choirs and other musical groups?
- Exercise or physical fitness groups?

- Recovery groups for people dealing with addictions?
- Support groups for single parents, those who have lost a child in death, divorced persons, ex-offenders, and others?
- Prayer and Bible study groups?

While groups that are part of the church's formal organization may not be entry points into the congregation for new people, they can nevertheless be an important part of the nurturing process for those who belong to them. Boards, commissions, committees, and councils can all be settings in which people grow closer to God and to each other. Task forces and mission groups may be able to reach out to and involve in their work people who do not yet have a formal connection with any congregation.

What Holds People Together

We've emphasized the importance of truly assimilating new people into the life of the church and of embracing diversity within the congregation. It's also helpful to think about some of the bonds that help hold people together—some of these are natural and some can be created. Some of the same factors that hold some people in the congregation together can also play a part in causing others to feel shut out.

Recognizing the existence of these factors can both help us take advantage of them within the congregation and also help us be sensitive to the barriers that they may cause for some people. This listing of factors that hold people together has been influenced by the observations of Lyle E. Schaller in his book *Assimilating New Members* (Nashville: Abingdon Press, 1978). Don't let the copyright on Schaller's book fool you; it's still an extremely valuable and relevant publication about assimilation.

As you go through this exercise, you'll become aware of some factors that bond people together and that force others out. Some of these are factors that cannot readily be changed, but being aware of them can be helpful. For example, if you have several people bonded together because of a strong position on an issue like war, abortion, or homosexuality, there may not be much you can do to change those positions (and you may not want to attempt to change them); but at least you can recognize and help them recognize the impact this may have on others who do not agree.

A Checklist of Factors that Hold People Together

Check those factors that are present for at least some people in your congregation. It will be very rare for a factor to be true for everyone in the same church, but you should be aware of those that apply to several in the membership and constituency.

_____ People who grew up in the same denomination as the church.

_____ People who grew up in the same congregation.

_____ People who are growing old together.

_____ People of who speak the same, non-English language.

_____ People of the same ethnic group.

_____ People who attended the same college.

_____ People who are in the same or similar careers.

_____ People who are related to each other.

_____ People attracted by or impressed with the current pastor of the church.

_____ People attracted by or impressed with a former pastor of the church.

_____ People attracted by or impressed with an associate pastor.

_____ People attracted by or impressed with a youth worker or the youth program.

_____ People attracted by or impressed with a Christian education director or the Christian education program.

_____ People attracted by or impressed with the music director or the music program.

_____ People who sing together in the choir or participate in the music program in other ways.

_____ People who have bonded with each other through work on a new church building or major improvements to the existing building.

_____ People who have bonded with each other through
a mission trip.

_____ People who have bonded with each other through
their involvement in a soup kitchen, an after-school
program, or another local service ministry.

_____ People who are bonded together because of their
strong positions on an issue like abortion, homosexuality, or peace.

_____ People who are bonded together because of their
political affiliation.

_____ People who are bonded together because of their
involvement in a support group, a Bible study
group, a prayer group, or another small group.

_____ People who are bonded together because of their
support of a war or their opposition to a war.

_____ People who are bonded together because they
are of the same social class.

_____ People who are bonded together because of their
unhappiness about something in the church: the
church's position on an issue, the pastor, the music,
the denomination, etc.

_____ People who are bonded together because of a strong
theological position (literal interpretation of the
Bible, interest in reincarnation, scholarly interpretation of the Bible, etc.).

_____ People who are bonded together because of intentional efforts in the church to create community.

_____ People who are bonded together because they share
in outreach to nonmembers.

_____ People who are bonded together because of their love
of the church building and location.

_____ People who are bonded together out of heritage and/or
nostalgia.

_____ Your addition: _____

_____ Your addition: _____

_____ Your addition: _____

Here are some important questions to consider as you think about the factors that hold people together in your congregation:

- What are the bonding factors that are most likely to attract new people to your church?
- What are the bonding factors that are most likely to cause guests to feel unwelcome in your church?
- What are the three or four bonding factors that affect the largest number of persons in your church?
- What additional bonding factors do you think would be beneficial for your church?

Back to Janice

Think back to the story of Janice with which this chapter began. Janice's relationship with the church was severely damaged by the judgmental perspective from which people viewed her unwed pregnancy. In a recent book by David Kinnaman and Gabe Lyons [*Unchristian*, Grand Rapids: Baker Books, 2007], the authors point out that young adults outside the church and inside the church are very bothered by the judgmental attitudes of many Christians:

> *Respondents to our surveys believe Christians are trying, consciously or not, to justify feelings of moral and spiritual superiority. . . . Nearly nine out of ten young outsiders (87 percent) said that the term* judgmental *accurately describes present-day Christianity.* [p. 182]

Closer relationships and true assimilation, especially of younger people, will not happen when judgmental attitudes are pervasive in a congregation. The best antidote to a judgmental environment is a true congregation-wide hospitality that runs both deep and wide.

The best small group programs in North America and the most highly organized evangelistic outreach efforts will not be successful if long-time members are judgmental in their view of others. It's easy for us to forget how much positive impact may be had by people of whom we may be inclined to disapprove. Consider, for example, the story of another unwed mother named Dorothy Day.

Dorothy Day had an abortion and then had a child out of wedlock. She was extremely poor, working for a very low wage and living in wretched housing. She was disillusioned with the institutional church, failing to understand why it did not do more to work for peace and justice and to feed the hungry.

But what Dorothy Day raised from the ashes of her painful and difficult life is a monument to the power of Jesus Christ and to the difference a committed person can make. She began *The Catholic Worker*, a penny newspaper, to instruct, counsel, motivate, and comfort people like herself who did not understand how the church could ignore the needs of the poor and participate so strongly in systems that harmed so many.

She opened soup kitchens to feed the hungry and started hospitality houses to care for the homeless, to clothe the naked, and to care for the sick. Circulation of her newspaper grew and grew. She co-founded the Catholic Worker Movement. Dorothy Day died in 1980, but the movement continues.

Dorothy Day's unwed mother status, horribly low income, and unconventional ideas brought her the disapproval of many. Yet

God worked through her in extremely powerful ways to change the Catholic Church for the better, to minister to the poor, and to work for peace.

There are many people outside the church today who have lost faith not in God but in what the church as an institution can do. Those feelings apply to Catholic, Protestant, and Anabaptist congregations. Many outside our churches are turned off by the judgmental attitudes of people who call themselves Christian. The same judgmental spirit that keeps many people out of the church also, at times, drives people like Janice away from the church. We can do better than this. We can practice a deep and wide hospitality that accepts people as they are, as blessings sent to us from God.

Chapter Eight
Creating Healthy Churches

1 Corinthians 12:12–14

Concept: There are no canned programs or quick fixes that will create the climate of hospitality in your church that will result in members who readily reach out to the unchurched and who can effectively assimilate new people into congregational life. Hospitality must run through the whole fabric of the congregation rather than simply being a welcoming "program," and the making of disciples must be a top priority for the church.

The Search for Happiness

Bonnie is thirty-four years old and had not been involved in the life of a church since her confirmation as a freshman in high school. It wasn't so much that she had bad experiences in the church as that she just didn't see the relevance of the church to her life. She focused her life on achieving success in her profession and on having a happy personal life. When her mother died this year at the age of sixty-two, Bonnie's view of the world was shaken. At first the death convinced her that God either did not exist or was not good.

Then she started looking at her mother's diaries and saw how much faith had influenced her mother's life. She thought back to things about God her mother had taught her when she was a little girl and in grade school. Bonnie decided to go back to church and found herself involved in a congregation with a food program for underprivileged children two afternoons a week. Bonnie started volunteering in the program, and she felt a pleasure and satisfaction that none of her other activities had given her. She was not "happy" in the sense that she had defined happiness before her experiences in the church and with the afternoon program, but she discovered a level of fulfillment that was richer than anything she had imagined before.

Tim, forty-two years old, was the service manager for a large automobile agency. He thought his life was happy and meaningful until the tenth year of his marriage. He came home from work one horrible summer evening to find his wife, his two children, the dog, and half the furniture in the house gone. His wife had left him a sad note, explaining that she had been trying to get him to deal with some of their problems for over a year but that he had continually glossed over them. Tim felt as though his heart had been cut out of his body. He was devastated; and the more he thought about it, the more he concluded that his wife was justified in what she had said and in what she had done.

A few weeks after his wife left him, Tim's next door neighbor invited him to go to church and then to brunch on a Sunday. It was perhaps the fifth or sixth time the invitation had been extended, and Tim had always felt before that he had no need of God or the church. This time Tim decided to accept the invitation. While he wasn't expecting much to happen as a result of visiting the church, he did think that he needed to make some changes in his life and thought it was worth a try. Going to church that Sunday changed his life. Tim felt his heart touched by the worship service and by the warmth of the people in the church. He continued going week after week, developed a deep faith in God, and truly found his life changed as a result. What he had thought was happiness before was nothing compared to how his life changed as he turned it over to God. In time he was even able to reunite with his wife and children.

Ann was fifty-one years old and had been a member at Saint Matthew's for five years. She had transferred her membership there from another congregation because of the excellent music at Saint Matthew's and because she had begun to feel bored in the other church. The same feeling of boredom, however, had begun to afflict her at Saint Matthew's.

A good friend of Ann who was also at Saint Matthew's shared this observation with her over a cup of coffee, "Ann, you view the church a lot like a restaurant. You choose the church that feels best to you; and if you start to get tired of the menu, you're ready to move on. But the church isn't like a restaurant, not really. You need to start thinking of yourself as being a part of the church, a member of the body of Christ. You need to roll up your sleeves and get involved. Join a Bible study group; participate in building a Habitat for Humanity home. You're so good at fixing things and making things. You redid your whole kitchen almost entirely by yourself. If you're bored with worship, tell one of the pastors what you'd like to see changed. Start seeing yourself as a part of the church, and you'll be amazed at how different you feel."

At first Ann was a little offended by what her friend had said. In the first place, she did think of the church a little like a restaurant; and she wasn't all that pleased with it at the moment. In the second place, her life was already full. Where would she get the time to join a Bible study group? To volunteer on one of the Habitat for Humanity homes that the church helped with two or three times a year? The more she thought about it, however, the more Ann began to wonder if she was missing something. She did join a Bible study group, and she joined others in working on the next Habitat for Humanity home. She didn't get around to talking with one of the pastors about worship because worship started feeling different to her than it had before. Finding time for things at the church no longer seemed a problem because Ann felt energized and fulfilled by what she was experiencing there. In fact everything in Ann's life felt better.

Bonnie, Tim, and Ann all experienced significant, positive changes in their lives through their involvement in a local congregation and the deepening of their personal faith. Another person helped prompt those experiences in each case: Bonnie's mother through her diaries, Tim's neighbor, and Ann's friend in the church. Deeper levels of involvement brought deeper faith and greater fulfillment for all three people.

There are new research initiatives to better measure individual and national well-being or happiness, but this is a difficult concept to quantify. How happy are people, and what makes them happy? In 1999, Ruut Veenhoven created "The World Database of Happiness," that includes ninety-five countries and rates average happiness on a scale from zero to ten based on several factors (http://www1.eur.nl/fsw/happiness/). At the time of this writing, Denmark is in the number one position with a score of 8.2; Canada is in eighth position at 7.6; the United States is in 17th position at 7.4.

The United States offers lots of choice and a high national standard of living, but there are big gaps between the rich and the poor, problems with nutrition, and fear of violence. Those factors caused happiness in the United States not to be rated as highly as in some other countries using Veenhoven's method.

There's some evidence that there may be a genetic component to positive well-being or happiness. Some people seem by nature to be more optimistic, more positive than others. There are also some for whom the glass is always half-empty rather than half-full and who seem to go through life in an almost constant state of disappointment or grumpiness! While it's virtually impossible to fully differentiate between the impact of genetics and the environment, it's not unusual to see strong similarities in outlook toward life in persons who are related to each other.

In one Christian Community study of young adults in North America, the desire for happiness was rated second only to the desire for safety and security. We have many people, both inside and outside our congregations, who want to be happy!

And that is an interesting situation for those of us who worship a God with nail-pierced hands. The Christian faith actually does not promise "happiness," or at least not as the world tends to define it. Faithfulness to the Gospel can certainly bring great joy and satisfaction, but it can also lead to the cross.

One of the challenges for congregational life is to offer people experiences and education that will help them have lives that are meaningful and pleasurable while also recognizing that following Christ can sometimes place us in uncomfortable situations. British lay theologian C.S. Lewis often used the word "joy" to describe the experience of a healthy relationship with Jesus Christ. Joy, as Lewis used the word, is something deeper and more permanent than happiness.

The church at its best offers people both a "safe zone" where they always feel welcome, love, and a deep sense of belonging and a "challenge zone" where they are encouraged to live in faithfulness to the Gospel. We need to embrace people with the kind of warm, healthy welcome that makes them want to keep coming and stay connected with the church. We also want to help them deepen their faith and their commitment to Jesus Christ. Bonnie, Tim, and Ann all developed greater closeness to God and an increased sense of well-being as they deepened their involvement in the church.

What Should the Church Look Like?

Many people have written extensively about what the church is becoming. There are books about being the church in a post-modern age. There are books that attempt to describe the emerging church. There are books that talk about the missional church. All these are thought-provoking, and a summary of all those themes goes beyond the scope of this particular book.

Based on Christian Community's studies of congregational life, we do have some observations to share concerning what healthy churches should look like—and what they should *not* look like.

1. Healthy churches take seriously helping people grow in their relationships with God. While many events in healthy churches will be entertaining and will help people be "happy," as our society views happiness, the center of life is to help people become better disciples of Jesus Christ.

Martha Grace Reese in *Unbinding the Gospel* (St. Louis: Chalice Press, 2006) writes:

> *Churches that emphasize a growing relationship with*
> *God for its members, board, and pastors are different*
> *than 'normal' churches. I don't want to sound critical,*
> *but visiting one of these vibrant churches makes attending*
> *many of our mainline congregations feel like going to a*
> *Lions Club meeting—a good thing, certainly, but not the*
> *real thing.* [p. 61]

What happens in worship services, in Christian education classes, in small groups, and in interpersonal relationships all works together to help people in their faith journeys in healthy churches.

People are living in a society that says to them that what they earn, what they own, and what authority or power they have are the factors that determine their worth and their importance. People are living in a culture of consumerism that says happiness is something that results from having a particular kind of house, furniture, car, clothing, or perfume. The Christian faith says that our identity is rooted in our relationship with God and that true meaning and purpose are related to our spirituality rather than to the standards of our society.

2. Healthy churches place a priority on prayer and see prayer as something that binds us both to God and to one another—rather than as a solitary pursuit. The deepest and best hospitality is nurtured and sustained through an emphasis on prayer. In *The Only Necessary Thing*, Henri J.M. Nouwen writes:

> *Prayer is the first and indispensable discipline of compassion precisely because prayer is also the first expression of human solidarity. . . . The Holy Spirit, the Spirit of peace, unity, and reconciliation, constantly reveals itself to us as the power through whom people from the most diverse social, political, economic, racial, and ethnic backgrounds are brought together as sisters and brothers of the same Christ and daughters and sons of the same Father.* [Crossroad Publishing, NYC, 1999, p. 61]

Pastors and church staff need to make prayer a priority. Church leaders need to make prayer a priority. And the entire congregation needs to be encouraged to develop a deep life of prayer—not just prayer for personal well-being but prayer for others in the community of faith, for society, and for the world.

Many people in our churches are uncomfortable with how to respond to people who seem different from themselves in significant ways. Older people may be uncomfortable with younger people who choose to live together before they are married. Younger people may fear the judgment of older people in a congregation and think that they need to withhold their opinions in church settings. In the Christian Community study cited in Chapter Six, 87% of the young adults who are church-active said that they "withheld their beliefs and opinions a significant amount of the time because they knew older members would disapprove of their views."

Heterosexual people may feel uncomfortable around people who are openly homosexual. And homosexual persons, who have experienced rejection and condemnation by many hetero-sexual Christians, may feel that the church is not a place where they can be open about a significant part of their identity.

People are often unsure how to relate to others of different ethnic or economic backgrounds. It's no accident that so many of our congregations are economically segregated as well as racially segregated!

People with significant mental, emotional, or physical challenges are often missing from our communities of faith. Our churches have not made their outreach and welcome process warm enough to involve those who face significant difficulties. And persons who deal with difficult challenges every day are not interested in the possibility of rejection or discomfort from a church.

Praying for others is the starting point for developing a deeper hospitality and a wider welcome for everyone in the body of Christ. Obviously we must move beyond prayer to action, but prayer can provide a foundation for positive actions and open our hearts to others. Pray for God to give you opportunities to reach out to others, and God will answer that prayer!

3. Healthy churches do not seek to make negativity the basic bond that holds people together. We are living in a time when a large number of congregations are heavily organized around negativity. Some churches form an identity that is heavily focused on opposition to abortion or homosexuality or stem-cell research or people living together before they are married or opposition to a particular political party. Those are certainly issues about which many people have very strong feelings, and it is appropriate for churches to help people relate their faith to such contemporary concerns. But when negativity becomes one of the major bonds holding people together, the result is rarely healthy. People who disagree with those strong opinions do not feel free to express that disagreement and in time simply drift away. A focus on negativism doesn't do much to open our hearts to the love of God for us and for all people.

4. Healthy churches avoid becoming identified with a particular political party. In the last twenty years, the United States has seen a growing number of evangelical and con-servative churches become heavily identified with the Republican party and with conservative political positions. The response to that from many mainline churches has been to move toward positions more in line with those of the Democratic party. Both of these directions are dangerous for the church.

Unquestionably the church should help people relate their faith to the decisions that they make and the values they hold. A Christian person should be influenced by his or her faith in determining for whom to vote in elections. But it is dangerous ground when a church starts pushing people in a particular political direction. Being part of the body of Jesus Christ is something much more than being part of the Republican or the

Democratic party! And the allegiance that we owe Christ transcends political party affiliations.

A healthy church should be able to have people of diverse opinions AND of diverse political party affiliations come together in worship and study. When a church becomes too identified with a particular political perspective, persons of differing viewpoints are either shut out or silenced. Salvation has not come in the past from any political party, and there is no indication that this will be the case in the future. We worship God, not political leaders.

This doesn't mean that churches should never take stands on issues of importance. But there is a significant difference between taking a stand on an issue and aligning with a particular political party or point of view on all issues.

5. Healthy churches seek to keep people from being hurt and from drifting away. There's an old saying in the southern part of the United States: "Ain't no hurt like a church hurt." The root of that saying is that damage people experience as part of a faith community can feel especially severe, like a betrayal. When people see the church as a safe and secure place in a world that is often troubling, it's horribly disappointing to experience pain and rejection.

Those who love us the most are also the ones who have the potential to hurt us the most. Acrimonious divorces stand as a strong example of this reality. In divorce, people who once loved each other so much that they wanted to spend the rest of their lives together decide that they can't stand each other. It's a painful journey to go from wanting to make love to someone to not even wanting that person to be in the same house. Family members, close friends, and church members are the ones with the greatest power to hurt us—precisely because we expect love and affirmation in those relationships.

As shared earlier in this book, people leave or drift away from the church for a variety of reasons:

- Sometimes people simply discover that the core beliefs within a congregation are simply too different from their own core beliefs. While a healthy church should be able to embrace people with a reasonably wide range of beliefs, there are times when the differences are just too great. When people leave a church for this reason, it's sad but not necessarily avoidable.

- Often people do not get deeply enough connected to the life of the church. The initial welcome that they experienced is not followed by deeper connections to others in the body of Christ.

- Sometimes people have unrealistic expectations of what being in the church will be like. There are some who expect that others will always agree with their opinions and who are hurt when that isn't the case. Sometimes a person joins the church thinking that the pastor or another staff member will become a new best friend, not recognizing that the pastor or staff member may have connections with hundreds of others in the church.

- People can experience relationship problems that are never resolved. They feel hurt by something that is said or by something that happens, and there is never any healing from that experience.

217

- People sometimes drift away because they do not develop a deeper discipleship through prayer, study, and involvement in the life of the church.

- And many people are lost because they break the habit of regular attendance during a time of vacation, of sickness, or of life interruptions and never return to regular involvement. When people say they don't know why they are no longer active in a church, they aren't always covering something up. Sometimes they truly do not know because they have simply drifted away. That will not happen, however, to people who have grown in the faith and who have deep and wide connections with others in the congregation. It also will not happen if people in the church notice the disruption in attendance and reach out to them.

How can those things be prevented? Here are some practical suggestions:

- Be sure that new member orientation encourages people to work toward deeper involvement in the congregation through Sunday school classes, prayer groups, small groups, service work, and in other ways. Also help people recognize that the church is a collection of sinners striving to be better rather than a collection of saints who have arrived at perfection. Don't hide the fact that people sometimes say hurtful things, but also encourage positive interactions with others.

- Assign faith friends or mentors to new members for the first one or two years of involvement in the church. Have a person or couple who work proactively to see that the new members meet others, become part of the social networks of the church, and find meaningful involvement in a class, small group, or service opportunity.

- Nurture class and small group involvement for everyone in the church.

- Monitor attendance and respond quickly when anyone breaks a regular pattern of participation at worship, Sunday school, a small group, or a service group. Christian Community studies have repeatedly shown that when churches follow-up on a change in attendance pattern within six weeks of the start of that change, the member returns to regular involvement 95% of the time. When the follow-up is delayed until six months after the start of that change, the probability that the person will return to regular involvement drops to 25%. The best initial follow-up is usually by telephone. A visit to the home can be an overreaction, and notes or cards are easily misunderstood. While a short e-mail can sometimes be effective in our technological age, remember that e-mails cannot convey nuance and, like a note or card, may come across as critical of the absence even though that was not intended. A visit to the home is always appropriate if the phone call doesn't result in a return to regular involvement.

- Encourage people to become involved in service projects, mission groups, or a board or committee of the church.

- Remember that the pastor and others on the church staff set the tone for how seriously everyone in the church takes the assimilation of guests and members. If the pastor and other staff model intentionality in moving people toward deeper involvement, others will pick up on that example.

6. Provide instruction in faith-sharing, hospitality, and assimilation to everyone in the congregation. Large numbers of people in our congregations know that they should share their faith with others and want to truly welcome and assimilate new people into the church but often do not know how to accomplish these tasks. Christian Community's congregational studies continue to show that growing churches differ from others in some significant ways related to hospitality and congregational life:

- 85.4% of those in the average congregation say their church is friendly to strangers and newcomers. In growing churches, however, 96.9% see their church as friendly to new people. Only 53% of those who visit the average congregation leave feeling that the congregation was friendly. In contrast, 88% of those who visit growing churches feel that the congregation was friendly.

- 65.7% of those in the average congregation say they take the initiative to talk to persons at church they do not know. The figure is 90.4% in growing congregations!

- 18.3% of the people in the average congregation identify cliques or exclusive groups that can make one feel unwelcome; that figure drops to 9.5% in growing congregations. In very unhealthy congregations, the percentage identifying cliques or exclusive groups may run over 50% of the active membership.

As the charts in Chapter Six showed, very few churches provide comprehensive training in outreach or in hospitality to constituents and members. Growing congregations are far more likely to do so. Several suggestions for training were provided in Chapter Six. Many churches have turned around their outreach through congregational-wide study of books like *Sharing Living*

Water, Widening the Welcome of Your Church, and the book you hold in your hands right now.

7. Healthy churches have an outward as well as an inward focus. Healthy churches take mission and service seriously. While they provide opportunities for worship, study, prayer, and nurture within the congregation, they also provide opportunities for outreach to the community and the broader world. The possibilities are numerous, and it's very likely that your congregation already has involvement in at least some of these opportunities:

- Providing or helping with a soup kitchen or a food pantry for the hungry.

- Providing shelter during the winter for those who are homeless (generally in cooperation with other churches and community agencies). Some communities and churches are seeking to provide shelter throughout the year–not just in the winter.

- Providing preschool or day care for young children.

- Providing after-school programs for children with opportunities for recreation, study, and meals.

- Providing youth group opportunities that reach out to teens who are not part of the church.

- Providing sexuality education for teens.

- Providing information on HIV/AIDS prevention to the neighborhood or community.

- Rehabbing homes for the elderly and for others with limited resources.

- Building or helping build Habitat for Humanity homes.

- Offering summer recreational programs for children.

- Offering summer camping and travel experiences for teenagers.

- Developing a relationship with a church or a mission program in another part of the world and helping that program through prayer, financial gifts, and volunteers.

- Offering marriage enrichment programs for couples in the community as well as in the church.

- Offering support groups for people who have experienced the death of a child, for the recently divorced, for single parents, and in response to other needs in the community.

- Sharing church facilities with organizations like Alcoholics Anonymous, scouting groups, and others who are making a positive difference in the lives of people.

- Develop an Educational Advocacy group to work for improved schools in your community.

- Develop a Stop the Violence group to seek strategies for lowering violence in your community.

- Develop a Peace for the World group to work for peaceful solutions in your community and to encourage legislators and leaders to work for peace in the broader world.

- Develop a Poverty Task Force to look at local and world poverty issues. The Task Force can work for programs and policies that will help alleviate poverty.

- Develop a group in the church to help both the church and its members and constituents live in more environmentally responsible ways.

- Develop a Denominational Connections Group that seeks to better understand the regional and national programs of your denomination. This can become an advocacy group for those programs within the church and can also become a feedback group to denominational organizations.

And so the list could be continued for many more pages. These opportunities not only help the church fulfill its mission as part of the body of Christ but also provide opportunities for people to grow in their discipleship and to become far more thoroughly assimilated into congregational life.

8. Become known as a church that truly practices a deep and wide hospitality, a church in which everyone is welcome. Many of our churches today are strongly segregated on Sunday morning in terms of race, economic level, physical ability, age, and sexual orientation. There is a tremendous need for churches that truly welcome everyone in the name of Christ.

There are certainly churches that grow by attracting people like those who are already part of the congregation. Some church growth strategies emphasize reaching out to those like the current membership of the church. Certainly there is nothing wrong with people reaching out to their friends, neighbors, and coworkers, who are indeed likely to be similar to themselves. They *should* reach out to those persons. But a church that takes the gospel seriously will also reach out to those who are different and will develop a hospitality that can cause very diverse people to feel welcome. Make that kind of hospitality a part of the core identity of your congregation, and you may be amazed by what happens in congregational life.

Indicators that People Are Assimilated

Many factors contribute to the level of a person's assimilation into the life of a congregation. If a person has other family members in the congregation and grew up in the denomination, that can certainly contribute to a high level of assimilation, but most new people are not likely to have family in the church and may not have a past denominational connection. The longevity of a person's membership in the congregation generally is an indicator of the level of the person's assimilation, but even those who have been in the church for years can come to feel that they are on the fringe.

The checklist that follows may be helpful to you in thinking about the level of assimilation of a particular participant or member. Feel free to photocopy the form. The checklist can be used in a number of ways:

- You can use it as a bulletin insert, encouraging everyone in the congregation to complete it for himself or herself and turn it in (without having to put a name on it). The tabulation of the responses by church leadership will help provide a better feel for how assimilated people are in the congregation.

- You can ask a faith friend or mentor of a new member or constituent to complete the form for that person. That can be a guide to the progress in assimilation that is being made.

- People who serve as deacons or caregivers can complete checklists for the persons assigned to them. This can then provide guidance in whether or not more initiatives should be taken to more fully assimilate those persons.

Obviously some of the items on the checklist, like attendance at worship, are very easy to complete for another person because records are available. A person completing the form for someone else may not know whether or not, for example, that person has demonstrated significant concern about the well-being of someone else in the congregation. Faith friends or mentors will likely be the ones who can most accurately complete the form for someone else, and of course people can do self-assessments with the form. Interpreting the meaning of scores on exercises like this one is in some ways always arbitrary, but these guidelines may help you:

Checked 10–12 items: This person is probably very well assimilated into the life of the church.

Checked 6–9 items: This person is reasonably well assimilated into the life of the church, but there is room for improvement.

Checked 3–5 items: This person is not well assimilated in the life of the church, and a faith-friend, mentor, deacon, or caregiver should be concerned.

Checked 0–2 items: This person is on the fringe of the church and will be likely to drop out completely if the level of assimilation is not improved.

Measuring Connection with the Church

Place a checkmark by each item that is true for you personally or for the person about whom you've been asked to complete the checklist.

_____ Attends worship three out of four weeks a month.

_____ Participates on a regular basis in a Sunday school class, small group, Bible study group, or similar weekly opportunity.

_____ Has at least six good friends in the congregation.

_____ Holds some kind of volunteer position in the church such as a committee membership, choir activity, ushering, or something similar.

_____ Takes the initiative to greet others that he or she does not know.

_____ Has brought a guest to worship or to another church activity at least once in the last year.

_____ Contributes financially on a regular basis. (The church treasurer or financial secretary can confirm this without revealing the specific amount.)

_____ Has a good relationship with at least one member of the church staff.

_____ Reflects positive feelings about the congregation in conversations.

_____ Reflects positive feelings about the denomination or about the broader outreach efforts of the congregation.

_____ Volunteers at least a couple of times a year to help with a service project or a fund-raising activity.

_____ Has in some way demonstrated significant concern about the well-being of someone else in the church.

Total number of items checked: _____

Deep and Wide

As shared in the first chapter, we've written this book out of concern that the level of hospitality in many of our congregations just doesn't go deeply enough to connect with people at a level that will keep them coming and isn't wide enough to help newer members really feel that they are as much a part of the community of faith as longer-term members. We're also aware that there can be long-time members of a church who do not feel deeply assimilated, who feel as though they are on the fringe of the congregation.

Hospitality cannot succeed if it is simply a program of the church, focused on warm smiles and handshakes at worship on Sunday morning. Warm smiles and handshakes at worship are certainly important, but hospitality needs to be part of the DNA of the congregation. People need to model a deep and wide hospitality in all that they do in the life of the church and as Christians in society.

We continue to live in a time when interest in spirituality on the part of people in North America is very high but interest in institutional churches is much lower. Yet people hunger for the kind of connection with God and the kind of meaningful community that the church at its best offers. We should take seriously the need to improve the quality of congregational life–not just because it will help our churches as institutions but because that is the way Christ wishes for us to interact with one another. The church as the living body of Christ has the potential to make a wonderful, positive difference in the hurting world in which we have been called to minister.

Resources

This list includes some publications to which reference was made in the book and other resources of which we want you to be aware. Those marked with an asterisk (*) are available through Christian Community/LifeQuest (www.churchstuff.com or 800–774–3360).

Boling, Ruth, *A Children's Guide to Worship*. Geneva Press, 2000. Helping children feel comfortable in worship.

*Bontrager Ed, *Building a Multicultural Congregation*. Fort Wayne: LifeQuest and New Life Ministries, 2003. A practical book with strategies for "widening the welcome of your church" to other cultures. This book talks about ways to develop inclusive worship, find the right leadership, share facilities with ethnic congregations, and begin a church of another ethnic group. This comes in a convenient notebook form with permission to photocopy.

Campolo, Tony and Gordon Aeschliman, *Fifty Ways You Can Share Your Faith*. Downers Grove: InterVarsity Press, 1992. Extremely practical ways you can reach out with Christ's love in actions as well as words.

*Clapp, Steve and Fred Bernhard, *Hospitality: Life in a Time of Fear*. Fort Wayne: LifeQuest, 2003. This book deals directly with the tough questions raised by the tragic events of September 11, 2001, and reveals that the answer to fear is not turning inward but turning outward. Learning to recognize the presence of Christ in others can have a liberating impact on all that we do and can enable us to move past the fears that threaten to immobilize us. This is an excellent guide to the development of hospitality as a part of the spiritual life and shows how hospitality relates to our faith, our homes, our neighborhoods, our places of work, and even our driving. Includes discussion questions for classes and small groups.

*Clapp, Steve and Fred Bernhard, *Widening the Welcome of Your Church*. Fort Wayne:LifeQuest, 1996, 1997, 1999, 2004. Can teaching people to share coffee and other forms of hospitality help a congregation grow? Coffee won't do it alone, but biblical hospitality will. That's what happened at the Oakland Church where 75% of the present worshippers were not present nine year ago. Attendance more than tripled, and the church continued to grow. This book places the Oakland experience in the context of strategies that have proven effective around the country in truly welcoming new people into existing congregations. This book has been so popular that it is now in its fourth edition and includes a study guide. Thousands of churches in North America have done congregational-wide studies using this book. ***Churches not comfortable with traditional evangelism will find many helpful strategies in this book and in the others by Steve and Fred.***

*Clapp, Steve and Fred Bernhard, *Worship and Hospitality*. Fort Wayne: LifeQuest, 2003. Looks at worship through the lens of hospitality. This book is an effort to move beyond the tension among traditional, contemporary, and blended worship to create worship which speaks to the deepest needs of people and builds up the church as the body of Christ. A guide for individual or group study is included.

*Clapp, Steve and Sam Detwiler, *Peer Evangelism*. Elgin: Brethren Press, 1993. Faith-sharing for teenagers. Designed for use in Sunday school classes, youth groups, or retreats.

*Clapp, Steve and Sam Detwiler, *Sharing Living Water*. Fort Wayne: LifeQuest, 1996, 2000, 2001. This book is an excellent companion to the one you are holding in your hands! While most church members readily agree that they should share their faith with others and invite them to church, many are not comfortable doing so. This practical, easy-to-understand book helps people identify the natural connecting points that give opportunities to share their faith or invite others to church without being manipulative or feeling awkward. The book discusses both verbal and nonverbal ways to share one's faith.

*Clapp, Steve, Carolyn Egolf, and Mary Ashworth, *Hospitality and Outreach in Christian Education: Practical Strategies for Sunday Schools, Small Groups, and Other Settings*. Fort Wayne: LifeQuest, 2008. This publication, being released a few months after the one you are now holding, looks at the place of hospitality and evangelism in the Christian education program of the congregation. The authors share the results of a research study that shows most congregations have failed to provide the training that would enable church growth through Sunday school classes, small groups, Bible study groups, youth groups, and other educational or spiritual formation settings. This is a very practical book, designed to have major impact on Christian education and congregational growth.

*Clapp, Steve, Kristen Leverton Helbert, and Angela Zizak, *Faith Matters: Teenagers, Sexuality, and Religion*. Fort Wayne: LifeQuest, 2003. Results of a comprehensive study of almost six thousand church-active teens, which looked at the relationship between their religious faith and their sexual behavior and values. The results of this study were released at a congressional briefing in Washington, D.C. Contains many practical suggestions for churches that want to improve their hospitality to young people and help them with decisions related to dating, marriage, and sexuality.

Delatte, Paul, *Commentary on the Rule of St. Benedict*. London: Burns and Oates, 1921. A classic work for those interested in this order and the practice of hospitality.

*Detwiler, Sam and Steve Clapp, *The Church of Recovery*. Fort Wayne: LifeQuest, 2002. Strategies for extending the hospitality of the church to persons who have problems with addiction. Recognizing the usefulness of the 12-step approach as a means of deepening the spiritual life for all people.

Frounfelker, Grace Moyer, *As a Little Child*. Scottdale: Herald Press, 1998. A great book on helping children feel welcome in the life of the church.

Hall, Eddy and Gary Morsch, *The Lay Ministry Revolution*. Grand Rapids: Baker, 1995. An outstanding book on empowering lay people for ministry and setting them free to do it.

*Helbert, Kristen Leverton and Dick Benner, *Public Relations Kit: Help from a Hospitality Perspective*. Fort Wayne: LifeQuest and New Life Ministries, 2003. Media exposure and publicity can play a valuable role not only in a church's evangelistic efforts but also in its outreach ministries. This practical kit, which comes with permission to photocopy, shares how the Internet, newspapers, radio, television, direct mail, the yellow pages, the telephone, the appearance of the church, and the attitudes of people can all contribute to the church as a place of hospitality.

*Hershey, S. Joan with foreword by Steve Clapp, *The First Thirty Seconds: A Guide to Hospitality for Greeters and Ushers*. Fort Wayne: LifeQuest and New Life Ministries, 1999, 2002, 2004, 2007. Greeters and ushers are the "first contact" with the congregation for many who visit. The number one question visitors want answered is: "Is this a friendly congregation?" This booklet offers clear training for greeters and ushers, with an emphasis on hospitality. Giving copies to all greeters and ushers in your church can help widen your church's welcome.

*Hershey, S. Joan and Steve Clapp, *Healthy Pastor–Healthy Church!* Fort Wayne: LifeQuest, 2003. Practical suggestions for improving the health and the effectiveness of pastors. Hospitality in the congregation should extend to the way in which pastors and their families are treated.

*Hershey, S. Joan, *Invite a Friend Kit*. Fort Wayne: LifeQuest and New Life Ministries, 2004, 2005. This kit will provide you with a thorough step-by-step action plan for an "Invite a Friend Sunday." The kit includes five copies of the booklet *A Guide to an Effective Invite a Friend Sunday* as well as a timeline for planning the event, ideas for engaging congregational participation, and sample printed resources.

Jarvis, Thea, *Every Day Hospitality: Simple Steps to Cultivating a Welcoming Heart*. Notre Dame: Green Press, 2007. This little book gives a delightful look at the kind of daily hospitality that should be an outgrowth of the Christian faith. It includes stories of hospitality from Thomas Merton, Dorothy Day, Mother Teresa, and others.

Keifert, Patrick, *Welcoming the Stranger*. Minneapolis: Fortress Press, 1992. This is an excellent overview of hospitality with special attention given to issues related to worship.

Kew, Richard and Roger J. White, *New Millennium, New Church*. Boston: Cowley Publications, 1992. (Cowley Publications, 28 Temple Place, Boston, Massachusetts 02111) Especially written from the Episcopal perspective but applicable to most mainline congregations and denominations. Very helpful in understanding the dynamics at work in most mainline churches.

Kramp, John, *Out of Their Faces and into Their Shoes*. Nashville: Broadman and Holman Publishing, 1995. This is the best contemporary book on faith-sharing we've seen except the one written by Steve Clapp and Sam Detwiler!

Mead, Loren, *Transforming Congregations for the Future*. Bethes-da: The Alban Institute, 1994. An insightful book—helping congregations move into the future. Emphasizes spiritual transformation and institutional change.

Miller, Herb, *Connecting with God*. Nashville: Abingdon, 1994. This is a wonderful book on nurturing the spiritual life of the congregation. You should have a copy.

Miller, Keith, *A Hunger for Healing*. San Francisco: HarperSan-Francisco, 1991. This ground-breaking book shows how the 12-step model relates to the classic spiritual disciplines and can be used to deepen the spiritual life. This book also communicates a great deal about authentic hospitality and caring.

Mortenson, Greg and David Oliver Relin, *Three Cups of Tea*. New York: Penguin, 2006. Mountain-climber Greg Mortenson drifted into a Pakistan village after failing to climb a mountain. The kindness of the people there moved him, and he promised to return and build them a school. This book tells the story of that promise and the extraordinary results–Mortenson built not just one but fifty-five schools, especially for girls, and did so in the terrain that gave birth to the Taliban. His efforts at relating to the people in Pakistan and to persuading people to donate the needed funds are a wonderful story about the impact of hospitality. The title comes from these words by a Pakistan village chief: "Here (in Pakistan and Afghanistan), we drink three cups of tea to do business: the first you are a stranger, the second you become a friend, and the third, you join our family, and for our family we are prepared to do anything–even die."

*Mundey, Paul, *Unlocking Church Doors: 10 Keys to Positive Change*. Nashville: Abingdon, 1999. While change is not the only factor that contributes to the vitality of a congregation, resistance to change can prevent a church from accomplishing its mission. Mundey provides a toolbox of ideas to help leaders transform their congregations.

Net Results. (308 West Blvd. N., Columbia, MO 65203) A bi-monthly publication offering new ideas for evangelism, church vitality, and leadership in each issue. This is an elecronic publication, coming in digital form. Originally associated with Herb Miller's outstanding work, the publication now reflects heavily the insights of Easum and Bandy. www.netresults.org

Peck, M. Scott, *Further Along the Road Less Traveled*. New York: Simon and Schuster, 1993. A book that has changed lives! Very helpful in understanding ourselves and others.

Peck, M. Scott and Marilyn Von Walder, *Gifts for the Journey*. San Francisco: HarperSanFrancisco, 1985, 1995. Many people seem unaware of this beautiful book on the Christian faith. Also available with an audio tape.

Posterski, Donald C., *Reinventing Evangelism*. Downers Grove: InterVarsity Press, 1989. A thought-provoking book which truly speaks to both the Canadian and the U.S. church.

Martha Grace Reese, *Unbinding the Gospel*. St. Louis: Chalice Press, 2006. This book has become very popular with leaders in several major Protestant denominations and offers a truly fresh look at how to do evangelism in the local church. The book includes a major emphasis on the place of prayer in evangelism and church growth.

Lyle E. Schaller, *Assimilating New Members*. Nashville: Abingdon Press, 1978. Don't let the copyright on Schaller's book fool you; it's still an extremely valuable and relevant publication about assimilation. The realities of how people are truly incorporated into the life of the church remain essentially the same, and Schaller offers very practical guidance.

Schaller, Lyle E., *Strategies for Change*. Nashville: Abingdon, 1993. If your church is struggling with change *or* if it needs to be struggling with change, this book will help!

Schaller, Lyle E., *The Very Large Church*. Nashville: Abingdon Press, 2000. Looks at the different issues involved in giving leadership to a large congregation including issues of relationships and hospitality.

Truss, Lynne, *Talk to the Hand*. New York: Gotham Books, 2005. There is a saying that goes, "Talk to the hand 'cause the face ain't listening." Truss deals with the reality that many people seem to have stopped listening and have stopped valuing basic courtesy and respect. She talks about examples of rudeness that range from the behavior of individuals in public places to the maddening depersonalization that so many businesses demonstrate in our time. This is not a religious publication, but the values which Truss mourns and would like to see receive renewed emphasis are certainly compatible with the Christian faith.

Study Guide:

Deep and Wide:

Hospitality and the Faithful Church

By
Kristen Leverton Helbert

Suggestions for Using This Study Guide

1. This study is suggested for use in adult Sunday school classes, Bible study groups, fellowship groups, church boards, lead teams, mission groups, or staff groups focused on improving the hospitality of the congregation. This *Guide* may also be used for individual study, but some suggestions are group-oriented.

2. Some sessions may offer more activities than time permits. Extra suggestions may be carried over to the next session, or you may choose those most suitable for your group's interests, needs, and size.

3. The *Guide* is designed for 8 sessions but may be used for a smaller or larger number of discussions, depending on your time. Choose the combination of topics most beneficial to your group. In some instances, you may want to scan the intervening material and share a short summary of it where needed to maintain continuity.

4. Remember that every group has both active and passive learners. Try to involve participants in a variety of ways, remaining sensitive to personalities and preferences. Encourage, but do not force, participation. Allow "I pass" as an acceptable response.

5. Having class members use different translations of the Bible will enrich your discussions and give new perspective.

6. Your leadership will be easier if you read the designated chapter in *Deep & Wide* and the accompanying session in this Guide before the time of the class or group meeting. There are also some sessions for which you may want to photocopy one or more pages from the book so that group members do not have to write in their books. The session plans assume that you will photocopy the indicated materials and that a chalkboard, whiteboard, or newsprint is available each week. Other needed preparation will be indicated in the session.

Session One:
Sylvester, Handshakes, and Expanding the Community

Items needed: one index card per person.

1. Hand each person an index card. Ask everyone to write down their *yes* or *no* responses to the following questions:
    *   Have you been hurt by the church or someone in the church?
    *   Have you ever considered leaving the church?
    *   Are their cliques or other exclusive groups within the church that make you feel excluded?
Collect the index cards, shuffle them, and redistribute them within the group. Ask the questions again, having class members raise their hands in response to the answers on the index cards they now hold. Ask class members if they are surprised at the perspectives that are shared.

2. This chapter reveals that "Within a year of officially joining a congregation, 62% of those members are *less active* in the church than at the time they joined. Twenty-five percent simply stop coming within the first year of official membership."
Why do new members become less active? Why do so many new members stop attending? What is one specific thing that you can do to improve these statistics in your congregation?

3. Summarize or read Steve and Sara's experience with Sylvester the cat at the beginning of this chapter. Do you believe that God arranges or intentionally brings new things into your life? If so, what does that say about how you respond to those who visit your church?

4. 1 Corinthians 12:12 from *The Message* by Eugene Peterson says, "You can easily enough see how this kind of thing works by looking no further than your own body. Your body has many parts—limbs, organs, cells—but no matter how many parts you

can name, you're still one body. It's exactly the same with Christ." Does your church function as the body of Christ or as individual parts? How should we approach visitors, new members, and long-time members if we are to view them all as parts of Christ's body?

5. Summarize or read the statistics shared in the section "Not as Friendly as We Think." Is your church friendly to newcomers? Do you go out of your way to talk to those you don't know well, including visitors as well as long-time members? Does your church care for one another in a way that is more compassionate than what people have experienced in other groups outside of the church?

6. Read the definitions of hospitality and the stranger on pages 21 and 22. What does "assimilation" of people within the congregation mean? Does your church extend hospitality to people who are already assimilated? Why do you think the authors decided not to put the word *assimilation* next to *hospitality* in the subtitle of this book?

7. Review the five points about hospitality that are made at the end of the chapter. Is hospitality a program or way of life within your church? What kind of labels do we put on visitors as well as long-time members? How can we work to erase those? Are the beliefs of your congregation clearly articulated and communicated to new persons who attend? Is your church reaching people from outside the church fold, or are you simply growing by gaining persons who have left other churches?

Optional Session: Invite persons who have recently visited your church, or persons who have recently left your church, to attend one session to share with the group their perception of the church and the welcome they received. If persons don't feel comfortable sharing with the group or are unable to attend, have a member of the group interview them and share those reflections with everyone.

Session Two:
A Biblical Look at Assimilation and Hospitality

1. Review the stories and life situations of Blake and Marcia (reduction in income and gifts to the church), Leslie (sexual orientation), and Bill and Ashley (felt like outsiders looking in on the church). Read Luke 10:27. How should this verse affect how we treat others?

2. Read Acts 2:42–47. How did the people in this passage treat one another? Were there acts of selfishness or selflessness? How did God reward them for their faithfulness?

3. Review or read the discussion of homosexuality in this chapter, which starts on page 31. Is human sexuality a topic that is discussed at your church? How should homosexuals be treated if we follow the mandate set forth in Luke 10:27?

4. Read Genesis 18:1–15. How did Abraham respond to the visitors? How would you respond today if three people arrived at your door, in need of food, shelter, and clothing? How should we respond to those in need in the community?

5. In the New Testament, Jesus provides several examples of how we are to treat others, especially those who are outcasts from society. The stranger does not have to prove the worthiness of his or her needs, but rather the responsibility is placed on the person who should faithfully respond to those needs. Read Matthew 26:6–13. Who are the "lepers" in our society? Are there people within your own church who are made to feel like outsiders?

6. Read Luke 10:29–37 and Luke 14:12–24. How diverse is your church economically? Racially? Socially? Generationally? In its worship elements? How might your church celebrate and embrace the diversity of God's creation that is talked about in these passages?

Session Three:
The DNA of the Inclusive Church

1. Read or review Darrell's story, which starts the chapter. How would it feel to be given the ultimatum, "Become a member or leave"? Our consumer culture fuels people's desires to have their own needs met, without necessarily thinking about the needs of others or thinking about making a difference in the lives of others. How do we balance the tension between meeting the needs of our visitors while also helping them to understand that the church is also for people with different needs?

2. Christian Community research reveals that only 23.8% of persons in the average church feel that "Our pastor(s) should spend as much time in ministry to unchurched people as to people in our church." However, 65.4% of people in growing congregations agree with that statement. How do you feel about your pastor(s) reaching out to the unchurched? How can you help to change the perspective of others in your congregation, so that the pastor(s) have adequate time and encouragement for reaching out?

3. Review the chart on pages 51 and 52, which lists 10 differences between new members and long-time members. Do you agree with all ten? Which do you disagree with? What differences are the most important? Which differences should be celebrated rather than ignored or extinguished?

4. Read or review the section titled "Is the Church Velcro or Teflon?" Is your church a Velcro or a Teflon congregation?
Why do you think that some issues are Velcro for long-time members when they are Teflon for new people? Name an instance from your church that may be Velcro for some and Teflon for others.

5. "Welcome one another, therefore, just as Christ has welcomed you, for the glory of God." Romans 15:7, NRSV. If the Gospel is for all people, what does that say about who we need to

reach out to? Are you too comfortable in the church setting? What sort of "evangelism" are you comfortable with? Consider stretching your comfort zone in order to invite someone new to attend a church function with you.

6. Read or review the section titled "A Positive Self-Image." How do members of your congregation perceive the church? Does your church have a positive or negative self-image? What positive, concrete steps can your congregation take to improve its self-image and to encourage growth?

7. Find the four obstacles to assimilation discussed in this chapter. Which are barriers in your congregation? Why do you think people are less loyal to denominations today? Have you ever heard the explanation "We've always done it this way!" when suggesting a new idea or program?

8. Review the nine characteristics of assimilated persons found on pages 77 and 78. How do you feel about your own assimilation into your church? What are things you can do to help others in their assimilation into your congregation?

9. Complete the "Who are the Forgotten?" chart at the end of the chapter. Can you identify one or two persons you know outside of the church that would match up with one or more of the categories you marked NC? Consider inviting them to a worship service, outreach activity, service project, or something else sponsored by your church to encourage their involvement.

Session Four:
The Price of Assimilation

Items needed: one index card per person.

1. This chapter starts with the statement that "There is a myth that small churches are just naturally friendlier and that large churches are colder." Do you agree or disagree? Why does this myth exist? What other factors play a part in the church being a friendly place?

2. "You are no longer strangers and aliens, but you are citizens with the saints and also members of the household of God." Ephesians 2:19. How does this verse apply to your life? How should you approach visitors on Sunday mornings?

3. Complete the "Do Guests Know You Are Expecting Company?" checklist for your church. Compare your responses with others, if applicable. What areas of hospitality can you identify that need improvement? How can you help bring about those changes?

4. "While we won't know every single person in a very large congregation, we most certainly want to know as many as possible. And names are important. Knowing the name of a person is a first step in understanding and valuing that person." What strategies can you use to remember the names of visitors and other persons within your congregation? How can you deepen the conversations you have with people? If general conversation with "strangers" doesn't come easily to you, what questions can you prepare ahead of time to ask so that you can engage in conversation and build relationships without feeling uncomfortable?

5. Consider the "Friendship Partners or Faith Friends" section of the chapter. Would this type of strategy work well in your congregation? Who have been your informal faith friends within

your church? Even without a specific friendship partner system in place, whom will you befriend?

6. Read or review the section titled "Worship and Transformation," noting the stories of (a) the forty-year-old woman whose mother had passed away; (b) the thirty-three-year-old gay man; and (c) the fifty-three-year-old woman who became a church participant through a quilting group. What elements should be included in worship services so that they are transformational experiences for those in attendance? How does hospitality play a role in transforming worship?

7. Read or review the section titled "Sharing Leadership." How readily does your church accept change? Are new members welcomed and integrated into leadership positions in your church? What can be done to diversify your church's leadership?

8. Hand each person an index card. Ask everyone to write down their *agree* or *disagree* responses to the following statements:
- Our church is open to change.
- I have been asked to be in a leadership role.
- The leadership of our church have considered and implemented ideas that I have suggested.

Collect the index cards, shuffle them, and redistribute them within the group. Repeat the statements again, having class members raise their hands in response to the answers on the index cards they now hold. Ask class members if they are surprised at the perspectives that are shared.

9. Look at the "Important Ratios for the Growing Church" on page 115. How does your church compare to the ratios suggested? Do you have ideas for new small groups to start that would improve the ratio of small groups to members? Do new members form at least seven friendships within the first six months of their attendance? Are there members of your church board (or leadership body) who have joined the church in the last four years?

Optional: Read or review the section titled "Membership Expectations." What expectations does your church have for new members? Are your expectations too high or too low for current members? How can you involve people, both new and long-time, who aren't involved beyond worship attendance? Should expectations of members be written out, or are those better left "understood?"

Session Five:
Spiritual Gifts and the Church

> In preparation for this session, you might find it helpful to have participants complete the "Spiritual Gifts Assessment" found on pages 129–141 in advance of the next meeting time.

1. Read the section titled "Spiritual Gifts Overview" and then review the seven qualities that spiritual gifts *are not*. Review the five qualities that spiritual gifts *are*.

2. Read 1 Corinthians 12. From the perspective of hospitality and assimilation, what verses stand out in this passage?

3. Complete the spiritual gifts assessment, found on pages 129–141. You may already have completed this assessment ahead of time. You are also encouraged to have someone else complete the assessment with your gifts in mind. This may be done before, during, or after this session.

4. Tally the results from your spiritual gifts assessment and discuss the results. Were you surprised by the spiritual gifts that were identified? How might you use your spiritual gifts in the life of your church?

5. Read or review the section titled "Spiritual Gifts and Assimilation." Does your church have a spiritual gifts process that includes long-time members as well as newcomers? If not, how might one be started? If so, are there improvements to be made? Are new persons being plugged into spots that match their spiritual gifts?

Session Six:
Children, Youth, and Young Adults

Options for this session: Depending on your church's situation and needs, you may decide to complete this session as written, or eliminate #4 (focused on children), #5 (focused on youth), or #6 (focused on young adults).

1. Brainstorm reasons why children, youth, and young adults do not attend churches in numbers as great as older adults. Draw from the situations and experiences of those you know in those age ranges who do not attend a church.

2. Read Matthew 19:13–15. What does this passage say about the importance of children in the life of your church?

3. Review the section titled "Evangelism and Hospitality Training," including the two charts, which show how few churches train their members in outreach and hospitality. Review the nine practical suggestions for strengthening your Christian education program. Complete the checklist that starts on page 153 and discuss the results. How prepared is your church to welcome and involve guests through your Christian education program?

4. Review the section titled "Strategies for Greater Hospitality to Children," including the fourteen key points. Which strategies have you already implemented in your congregation? Which should you implement or improve on?

5. Review the section titled "Strategies for Greater Hospitality to Youth," noting the seven specific suggestions. What issues do you remember facing during your youth? Which strategies have you already implemented in your congregation? Which should you implement or improve on?

6. Review the section titled "Strategies for Greater Hospitality to Young Adults," paying special attention to the ten issues which

young adults and older adults have differing opinions on. Why do you think people of different ages have different opinions on church and societal issues? Review the eleven strategies for improving hospitality to young adults. What strategies have you already implemented in your congregation? Which should you implement or improve on?

7. Close with prayer, thanking God for all of the people in your congregation and those who will become part of your congregation in the future.

Session Seven:
Ports of Entry and Deeper Relationships

1. Read or review the story of Janice which starts the chapter. How would Janice be treated in your congregation? What life situations might represent a challenge to your membership?

2. Read or review Brad and Mary's story. How can you seek to be proactive so that similar situations don't happen at your church?

3. Read Acts 2:42–47, which was also studied in chapter 2. How has your perspective changed on this passage since having read more in this book?

4. Review the five suggestions made under "Building Relationships in Groups." What specific steps can your congregation take to improve the groups within your church? Brainstorm on what new "mission groups" can be added. Should (additional) small groups be formed?

5. Review the section titled "Foyer—Living Room—Kitchen Table." How does your church do in assimilating new and long-time members? What stage are most members assimilated to? How can you work to make sure that all persons are "around the kitchen table?"

6. Review the section titled "A Primer for Starting Small Groups." Do you think it's better to have separate groups for new people or to integrate them into existing groups? What should be done to start or improve the small group ministry of your church?

7. Review the four ports of entry that are discussed towards the end of this chapter. Brainstorm a long list of ports of entry that exist and that can be created within your church.

8. Complete the "Checklist of Factors that Hold People Together." How did your church fare? What areas can be improved?

Session Eight:
Creating Healthy Churches

Items needed: one index card per person.

1. Read or review the section titled "The Search for Happiness." Give each participant a notecard and have them list sources of happiness on the left side of the card and barriers to happiness on the right side of the card. Have participants share, as they are comfortable, what they wrote on their cards. How can being aware of what makes us unhappy be a healthy thing?

2. Read 1 Corinthians 12:12–14. What does this passage say about the importance of each member of your group?

3. The first two key points made under the section "What Should the Church Look Like?" are:
- **Healthy churches take seriously helping people grow in their relationships with God.**
- **Healthy churches place a priority on prayer and see prayer as something that binds us both to God and to one another—rather than as a solitary pursuit.**

How does your church help everyone grow in their relationship with God? Is there an emphasis on prayer in your congregation?

4. The second two key points made are:
- **Healthy churches do not seek to make negativity the basic bond that holds people together.**
- **Healthy churches avoid becoming identified with a particular political party.**

Are their negative opinions on issues that are strongly held by your congregation? What can be done to lessen the effects of that negative climate? Is your church closely identified with a political party? What are the drawbacks of being closely aligned with any one party?

5. Review the discussion that follows the fifth key point about healthy churches:

- **Healthy churches seek to keep people from being hurt and from drifting away.**

If you are comfortable, share how you or someone you know has been hurt by the church (being careful not to share gossip or to complain, but simply sharing a situation that has happened). How can you help those who have been hurt by the church to heal and to feel fully included again?

6. Complete the "Measuring Connection with the Church" checklist found on page 226. Share the results of your checklist. Were you surprised with your level of assimilation? With the level of assimilation of others in your group?

*About Christian Community
And LifeQuest*

Christian Community and the publishing imprint of LifeQuest are committed to finding practical strategies that help churches with the pressing issues of our time. We do careful research and field-testing so that we know the strategies we offer will work in churches like yours. We have no interest in manipulation, gimmicks, or overly simplistic answers to complex problems.

Our research and development projects have been concerned with topics such as:
- Improving the hospitality of congregations
- Developing strategies for improved congregational outreach
- Relating stewardship directly to the spiritual life
- Expanding opportunities for planned giving to local congregations
- Conducting congregational surveys and helping churches and judicatories relate the survey information to strategic planning
- Helping churches move beyond tensions between contemporary and traditional approaches to worship
- Understanding how the religious faith of teens relates to their sexual values and behavior
- Developing strategies to help congregations do more with sexuality education and marriage enrichment not only for teens but for people of all ages
- Helping congregations become more welcoming to all people, regardless of race, economics, physical ability, sexual orientation, or gender identity
- Understanding the different ways that young adults and older adults view the church and society

We are also committed to cooperative work with others. We have involved churches of over thirty different denominations in our research and development projects, and we often work cooperatively with regional and national denominational officials. We have continuing partnerships with New Life Ministries; the Religious Institute for Sexual Morality, Justice, and Healing; and the Network for Charitable Giving.

To order resources or for more information about our organization, you can contact us at:

Christian Community, Inc.
6404 S. Calhoun Street
Fort Wayne, Indiana 46807
800-774-3360 (for orders)
260-456-5010 (for information)
DadofTia@aol.com
www.churchstuff.com

More on Hospitality from Christian Community

The First Thirty Seconds: A Guide to Hospitality for Greeters and Ushers by S. Joan Hershey.

Widening the Welcome of Your Church by Steve Clapp & Fred Bernhard.

Hospitality: Life in a Time of Fear by Steve Clapp & Fred Bernhard.

Hospitality and Outreach in Christian Education: Practical Strategies for Sunday Schools, Small Groups, and Other Settings by Steve Clapp, Carolyn Egolf, and Mary Ashworth.

Invite a Friend Kit by S. Joan Hershey.

Public Relations Kit: Help from a Hospitality Perspective by Kristen Leverton Helbert and Dick Benner.

Building a Multicultural Congregation by Ed Bontrager.

Worship and Hospitality by Steve Clapp & Fred Bernhard.